There's More Than One W

Don't Wait—Anticipate

Watch your dog's body language and recognize how certain behaviors—such as sniffing, scratching, or circling movements—indicate specific needs.

Work Smarter—Not Harder

Create schooling sessions that combine positive feedback ("Good dog!") and redirection ("Outside!"). It will save time and help you understand how your dog learns.

Get to Know Your Dog

Does he like to play games, learn tricks, or go on walks? Discover what motivates your dog, then design lessons to fit his personality and stimulate a desire to learn.

Teach Any Dog New Tricks

Dogs learn faster when owners work on more than housetraining with them. In addition to mastering the house rules, dogs can learn to walk wearing a leash, come to you, sit down, sit up and beg, and roll over.

Together—You Can Both Do It!

Krista Cantrell, a cognitive animal behaviorist, is a frequent speaker and clinician who describes her training methods as "dog-friendly." Her unique no-force training methods grew out of a lifetime spent listening to animals and learning how to see the world through their eyes. With more than twenty years' experience, she has developed her own dog-training philosophy, emphasizing experiential learning, behavior modification, and playSMART® techniques. She is the author of *Catch Your Dog Doing Something Right* (Plume). She lives in the high Sonoran Desert of Arizona with her husband, two dogs, cat, and six horses.

ALSO BY KRISTA CANTRELL

Catch Your Dog Doing Something Right

Housetrain Your Dog Now

KRISTA CANTRELL

A PLUME BOOK

PLUME
Published by the Penguin Group
Penguin Putnam Inc., 375 Hudson Street,
New York, New York 10014, U.S.A.
Penguin Books Ltd, 27 Wrights Lane,
London W8 5TZ, England
Penguin Books Australia Ltd, Ringwood,
Victoria, Australia
Penguin Books Canada Ltd, 10 Alcorn Avenue,
Toronto, Ontario, Canada M4V 3B2
Penguin Books (N.Z.) Ltd, 182–190 Wairau Road,
Auckland 10, New Zealand

Penguin Books Ltd, Registered Offices:
Harmondsworth, Middlesex, England

First published by Plume,
a member of Penguin Putnam Inc.

First Printing, February, 2000
1 3 5 7 9 10 8 6 4 2

playSMART and Animal Energetics are registered service marks
owned by Krista Cantrell.
Bitter Apple, Buster Cube, Kong, and Frisbee are registered trademarks.

Ⓟ REGISTERED TRADEMARK—MARCA REGISTRADA

LIBRARY OF CONGRESS CATALOGING-IN-PUBLICATION DATA
Cantrell, Krista.
Housetrain your dog now / Krista Cantrell.
p. cm.
ISBN 0-452-28160-1
1. Dogs—Training.   I. Title
SF431.C365   2000
636.7'0835—dc21   99-043790

Printed in the United States of America
Set in Souvenir
Designed by Eve L. Kirch

For Kate and JoAnn, allies in the world of words.

In memory of Trevor, 1984–1998; the best golden re-trevor ever.

Acknowledgments

How many ways can I say thank you? The following people and dogs deserve special mention. Four paws up to:

Debby Boehm; Kate Kling, Ph.D.; and JoAnn White; who keep me on track.

Jennifer Dickerson Kasius, my editor.

Michael Larsen and Elizabeth Pomada, my agents.

The following clients whose dogs posed for photographs: Sandra Baskin and Zak (West Highland white terrier); Fran Charlton and Sir Spencer Tracey (Miniature pinscher) and Lady Katey Hepburn (Chihuahua); Sandra Michael and Cody (Doberman pinscher); Helen Parkhill and Sunny (Australian shepherd); Trish Prescott and Luke Skywalker (Labrador); Debby Ryan and Stutz, Sierra, Harmony, Mercedes (Saint Bernards), and Zoey (bulldog); Terry Schumacher and Chief (Dalmation); JoAnn White and Ashley (standard poodle).

Jeff Cantrell, husband extraordinaire.

And my best friends, the dogs in my life, Trevor and Red Sun Rising C.D.

Contents

Preface

I picked up the phone after two rings. "Hello, this is Krista Cantrell." A violent sneeze and two loud sniffs answered me. "Can I help you?"

The woman cleared her throat, paused, then words drained out of her like dirty water after pulling a plug in a sink.

"My name is Nancy. My carpet cleaner gave me your name. You have to see me right away; I can't take it anymore. I went to the animal shelter to drop off my dog, but I couldn't go inside. Instead, I sat in my car in the shelter's parking lot with my little shih tzu on my lap and cried for the past hour. I just couldn't leave him. But the other trainer I worked with didn't help us. I don't know what to do. You are my dog's last chance."

"What's wrong?" I asked.

"Rambo is six," Nancy said. "I've only had him for a year. The people at the shelter said he was there because the couple who owned him was getting a divorce, but no one told me he wasn't housetrained!"

"How long has your dog been soiling in the house?"

"Ever since I brought him home. At first, he only had an accident once a week, but now he's going at least three times a week behind the sofa and in the corner of the family room. Yesterday, my three-year-old niece stepped in a pile and dragged it through my dining room, living room, family room, kitchen, and bathroom. My whole house reeked. That's when I called the carpet cleaner, and he said I should call you immediately. Can you help me?"

"Yes," I assured her, "we can solve this problem."

Housetraining your dog is the most important behavior you will ever teach. It can challenge your time, resources, patience, and imagination. Fortunately, housetraining can also be easy, fun, and rewarding for you and your dog.

Housetraining is more than waste product control; it's the first step in building a relationship with a dog. Your attitude toward housetraining and the methods you use can help or hurt your other dog-training efforts.

As a cognitive animal behaviorist, I am frequently the last alternative in a person's search to solve distressing housesoiling problems, such as papertraining two Dachshund littermates at the same time, schooling a resistant schipperke, or finding effective alternatives for an older, almost incontinent, German shepherd.

In my search to find training techniques that worked, I discovered that the critical factors in teaching dogs where to eliminate were the *handler's* attitude, lifestyle, and dedication rather than the dog's breed, size, or temperament.

As the handler, the hard part is that you are all alone with no one to cheer you on while you teach your dog to target a particular location for his puddles or piles. At one o'clock in the morning as you wait for your puppy to do his business in the yard, the cool night air whistles through your flimsy cotton robe. After a hard day at work, you take your Scottie, Chip, for "the walk" before you even change clothes. At night, instead of watching your favorite television show, you are looking at Chip as he searches for the right bush to mark.

Three perfect, accident-free days pass. Then on Wednesday your work schedule changes; you must work an extra two hours every day. Friday, your best friend flies in from Syracuse for a long weekend. You skip Chip's early morning walks, feed him late on Monday night, and early on Tuesday morning. Tuesday night when you arrive home, you are greeted by a bouncy Scottie and two piles on the oriental rug under your dining room table.

A high shriek escapes your lips. "This has got to stop! Why isn't this dog housetrained?" After all, you had a plan. You can't help it that your best friend visited for four days and you had to work overtime during the week. Now every day you find piles on the oriental rug. Today, after you took off your shoes, you accidentally stepped in a wet spot next to the bed.

Housetrain Your Dog Now removes the questions, doubts, and frustrations from the housetraining process and replaces them with knowledge, understanding, and confidence. Easy solutions provide answers when you find yourself shouting, "There must be a better way to housetrain a dog!"

In exchange for 14 days or less of your time, you can have an "accident-free" dog. *Housetrain Your Dog Now* shows you how to find time to train, and make the most of this time, by understanding how dogs learn, setting priorities, finding assistants, and using behavior-based rewards for fast results. Practical step-by-step solutions are tailored for city, suburban, or country lifestyles.

Part 1, "Get Ready!" explains five factors that affect dog behavior; four ways to maximize your housetraining time; and how the right tools and equipment make housetraining easier. It covers the difference between papertraining and housetraining and helps you decide which one is right for you.

Part 2, "Get Set!" describes housetraining methods appropriate for city, suburban, or country dogs; the building blocks of learning; how rewards change behavior; why punishment does not work; six rules that speed up learning; and how to design an effective housetraining schedule.

Part 3, "Go!" explores exercises, tricks, and games to speed up the housetraining process. In addition, it covers how to re-train the resistant dog, and describes solutions to 14 common housesoiling problems.

The following symbols alert you to special Habit Forming Tips, Helpful Hints, Important Points, and Time Savers.

 Habit Forming Tip

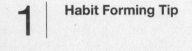

 Important Point

 Time Saver

Taking more than two weeks to housetrain your dog is like water-skiing behind a bass boat instead of a ski boat. Although a bass boat gets you up and out of the water, the ride is slower, longer, and not as much fun. My advice in *Housetrain Your Dog Now* is based on proven methods of housetraining dogs that bring results in just 14 days. The best part is that by the third or fourth day, the dog starts understanding what you want, and the teaching gets easier, not harder. Many of my clients find that by the sixth or seventh day, their only job is to reward the dog for puddles and piles in the right place. And that's easy. No stress. No fuss. It's fun to reward a clever canine with games, walks, toys, food, or praise.

Housetrain Your Dog Now shows you how to *enjoy* house-training your dog. To prove it, just read on.

PART 1

Get Ready!

CHAPTER 1

● ● ● ● ● ● ● ● ● ●

What Every Dog Handler
Should Know

Heavy with sleep, my eyelids struggled to open. I looked at the alarm clock: 2 A.M. Too early to get up. I turned to my side and large hazel eyes peered at me. "What is it, Trevor?" I asked my yellow golden retriever. "It's not time for our morning walk yet. Go to sleep."

Trevor did not budge from his position next to the bed, but continued staring at me, his signal that he needed to go outside.

"Outside? Do you need to go outside?" I asked.

Trevor turned and walked to the foot of the bed.

"Just a minute, let me get my robe on."

Silently we went downstairs. I flipped on the outside lights, opened the sliding glass door, and said, "Trevor, go on, go on."

Watching from the kitchen window, I saw Trevor trot out and pee. A huge, yellow stream cascaded to the ground; it could not have waited four more hours until morning.

The golden boy has done it again, I thought. Even though the stairs were difficult for my 13-year-old golden retriever to navigate with his arthritis, he climbed the steps to reach our bedroom. Without realizing it on that early Tuesday morning, Trevor demonstrated the three behaviors that successfully housetrained dogs know.

Behavior #1. Dogs "tell" you when they need to go outside.

Behavior #2. Dogs empty their bladders or bowels on your request.

Behavior #3. Dogs eliminate in the correct location without any supervision.

Target a Toilet Area in Just 14 Days!

Successful housetraining requires the active participation of you and your dog. The 14 days it takes to teach a dog the house rules is quite small in comparison to the average dog's 10-year or 3,650-day life span. In only 14 days you have the opportunity to reinforce a puddle or pile in the right spot at least 70 times. This is more than enough time for a dog to link a signal—"go potty"—to a behavior—emptying of a bladder or bowel—to a food, game, toy, or walk reward. But that's not all! During this time you can develop a relationship that will broaden your perspective of what it means to be best friends with a dog. Housetraining is a process that is influenced by many events. Before you start your housetraining program, consider the following five factors that influence dog behavior.

Five Factors That Affect Dog Behavior

You can housetrain your dog, I promise. However, your understanding of why, when, and where elimination occurs is critical. When you learn to recognize the specific dog behaviors that precede puddles and piles, the quickest way to target a toilet area, and effective techniques to link rewards to behavior, you can create schooling sessions that will facilitate your dog's housetraining.

FACTOR #1: THE DOG'S AGE

Puppy bladders are tiny, and puppies must urinate frequently. By eight and one-half weeks, puppies search for a specific location for puddles and piles. This is a perfect time to begin housetraining, since puppies usually eliminate every one or two hours until they are 12 weeks old.

In the case of the adolescent or adult dog who needs retraining, age is not the issue. The dog can control his sphincter muscles or bladder. Instead, the problem is that the dog's initial housetraining was incomplete. As a result, the dog never adopted your house rules as his.

Older dogs who are incontinent know what they are supposed to do, i.e. eliminate outside, but they are incapable of controlling their bodily functions. One of the best ways to work with older dogs is to develop a schedule for eating and bathroom breaks that fits their cycle of elimination. In addition, you can replace carpet with tile, use doggy diapers, or place "doggy pads" underneath them while they rest.

FACTOR #2: AMOUNT OF SUPERVISION

Twelve-week-old Lhasa apsos, 6-month-old collies, 5-year-old Irish setters, and 13-year-old Afghans require more than your physical presence. They demand your *mental attention* as well. You must actively participate in their teaching program.

Nancy, one of my clients, bought a miniature schnauzer, Cassius, before she was diagnosed with Epstein Barr. Because of Nancy's illness, she rarely left her bedroom. Most of the time, Cassius would lie curled up next to Nancy in bed, but frequently when Nancy woke up from a nap, Cassius was nowhere in sight.

Nancy did not close her bedroom door, but allowed Cassius to roam throughout the house. Nancy believed that Cassius would not eliminate inside the house if she was home, but she was wrong. The call of nature cannot be ignored; instead it must be anticipated!

Nancy followed the same routine every day. She brought Cassius outside to the backyard toilet area after he ate his breakfast, lunch, and dinner. However, Cassius needed to eliminate more frequently than three times a day, so he used the corners of the living room, dining room, and guest bedroom as his special toilet areas.

Nancy learned that responsibility does not stop even if you are sick, tired, or busy. Dogs who are not housetrained demand your active participation and supervision unless they are confined.

1 | **Habit Forming Tip:** Successful housetraining requires your physical and mental presence. Prevent accidents by watching your dog when he runs free. Only with constant observation can you learn your dog's body language and recognize how certain behaviors indicate that he needs to eliminate, such as sniffing, scratching, or circling movements.

FACTOR #3: HEALTH AND MEDICATION PROBLEMS

Health and medication problems can hit at any time. The best way to recognize when you need to call a veterinarian is to know how your dog normally looks and acts, as well as how much she eats and eliminates. Then you can recognize a difficulty when it first starts. Stay alert. Call your veterinarian as soon as you suspect a physical problem. Bacteria, viruses, fungi, and parasites can seriously impair your housetraining program. For example, blood in the urine can indicate a urinary bladder infection, kid-

WHEN TO VISIT THE VETERINARIAN

Signs

Coat—dull, matted, clumped hair, or bald patches
Skin—lesions, scaly areas, sores, redness, bare spots
Eyes—watering, milky, yellow, or green mucus, ulcers
Ears—dirty, smelly, waxy, red
Nose—dripping, hot
Stomach—bulges, spasms
Anus or vulva—discharges, hair loss, redness

Conditions

Physical distress such as: bleeding, difficulty breathing, continual vomiting or diarrhea, lack of appetite, constipation, high temperature, excessive coughing or sneezing, constant licking at anus or vulva, scooting on rug, increased drinking or urination, straining to urinate or defecate, or blood in urine.

ney infection, stones or crystals in the bladder, as well as a bacterial, fungal, or parasitic infection. Medications can have side effects, including diarrhea, constipation, excessive urination, and decreased or increased appetite. A veterinarian can determine the cause of the problem and give you the appropriate diet, medication, or remedy to resolve it.

2 | **Habit Forming Tip:** Schedule a physical examination for your dog at least once a year.

FACTOR #4: PRESENCE OF OTHER ANIMALS

Gary called me after his smoothly running household of three cats and one corgi was disrupted by the addition of a border ter-

rier, Keenan. Now puddles and piles made appearances on sofas, carpeting, and in the closet. After he found a wet spot on his
bed, Gary knew he needed help. Although Gary had lived with
dogs his whole life, this was his first terrier. Keenan was an 18-
month-old intact (not castrated) male whose breeder stopped his
show career and placed him as a pet dog. However, when Gary
brought Keenan home, Keenan chased cats! He urinated on the
edge of sofas and table legs, and left piles on the tile floor. Now
it seemed that the cats and corgi had joined in and were spraying their scent over Keenan's puddles and piles.

Gary had assumed that because Keenan was 18 months old
and a show dog, he was housetrained and good with other animals. When Gary brought Keenan home, he opened the door,
unsnapped Keenan's leash, and let him go. However, Keenan
had spent his life enclosed in kennel runs. He had never lived inside a house. Keenan pooped on the tile instead of grass because the kennel run he grew up in had cement floors. Dogs
develop favorite surfaces for leaving their puddles and piles, and
to Keenan, the tile's surface felt similar to cement.

Gary could not understand why his corgi and cats lost their
perfect manners after Keenan joined the family. I explained to
him that border terriers are friendly, active dogs who can be
scrappy and independent. Originally bred to hunt foxes, bad-
gers, and rats, they have sharp chasing instincts. It made perfect
sense that due to Keenan's breeding, he chased cats. Keenan's
fast entry into Gary's house accentuated Keenan's survival instincts. An introduction on neutral territory or a slow introduction through the use of crates, gates, and closed screen doors
would have allowed Keenan to meet the corgi and cats in more
neutral circumstances. Instant face-to-face confrontations often
threaten the best of animals. Dogs and cats need time to adjust
to each other. Once Gary understood that his corgi and cats felt
threatened, we were able to design an action plan to correct the
situation.

FACTOR #5: STRESS LEVEL

Dogs often encounter stressful events in their day-to-day existence. Sirens, fighting between family members, thunderstorms, loud music, uneasy relationships with other dogs or cats, or deaths in the family of animals or people are possible tension builders.

Anxious, uneasy, or tense dogs often suffer from digestive upsets, diarrhea, loss of appetite, vomiting, infections, and nutritional deficiencies. Dogs who are stressed cannot relax. Dogs who cannot relax do not allow their bodies to rejuvenate, and often experience bathroom breakdowns.

3 | **Habit Forming Tip:** Working with a dog is like building up a savings account. When you deposit patience, understanding, and fun, you compound the dog's interest. Remember, in order to make a withdrawal, you must first make a deposit.

Get Ready to Housetrain Your Dog

Housetraining is not an isolated event such as, "Oh good. My dog is housetrained. Now I can teach her to heel on leash, roll over, and come." The relationship you establish while housetraining your dog starts, stops, and grows every other behavior. The following steps will help you to nurture your dog through the housetraining process, develop a happy and responsible family member, and improve your ability to teach other dog behaviors.

STEP 1: BUILD THE RELATIONSHIP

The way you approach housetraining—what you do, how you react to the dog, how the dog responds to you—sets the tone for every interaction with your dog *for the rest of the dog's life.* For example, if your Jack Russell terrier, Brinkley, has an accident and you yell, hit, or rub his nose in the pile, he may hide, run away, or cower when you come home from work. Brinkley will connect your presence with punishment, not with his pile under the dining room table.

You think you are reprimanding Brinkley for the pile on the floor; he thinks you are crabby. Most of the time, Brinkley "hides" puddles or piles from you to avoid getting punished. Now, it will be more difficult to housetrain him because if you do not see the behavior, you cannot work with it. Later, when you call Brinkley's name after you arrive home, he may hesitate. Brinkley may no longer eagerly greet you, but instead watch and wait to see if you will suddenly get angry at him "for no reason."

Every interaction you have with a dog builds or diminishes your rapport. How you work through and help Brinkley with toilet training affects how he listens to you; your ability to teach sit, down, come, heel, or stay; and your effectiveness at solving behavior problems such as barking, jumping, or running away.

STEP 2: FIND THE RIGHT APPROACH

Housetraining a dog requires that you determine what makes your dog tick. Does your dog like to play games, learn tricks, or go on walks? Once you understand what motivates your dog, then you can design lessons to fit the dog's personality and stimulate his desire to learn.

Your challenge is to match your expectations with the dog's needs. The teaching method you used with your last dog may not work with your new dog. Your lifestyle—where you live, the hours you work, the presence of other animals or people, how often you travel—affects what you teach and how you teach it. For example, five years ago you papertrained your bichon frise because you lived alone in a third-floor apartment in Boston. Now, you are married with two children and live in the suburbs. You don't want to papertrain your chocolate Labrador. He's too big. Besides, he has easy access to the backyard through a doggy door. Different situations require different solutions. There's more than one way to train a dog; use housetraining methods that fit your current lifestyle and environment.

4 | **Habit Forming Tip:** Find out what makes your dog unique. Discover what makes your situation different. Use housetraining methods geared to your lifestyle.

STEP 3: DON'T WAIT—ANTICIPATE!

Housetraining happens easily and naturally because dogs pay close attention to where they eliminate. Dogs don't randomly "go" somewhere, they *choose* a specific location. However, your actions can influence your dog's decision

Housetraining requires that you are aware, attentive, and alert to the signs and signals that your dog needs to eliminate. For example, if a puppy or dog starts sniffing and circling in the corner of the living room away from his food and bed, stop fixing dinner, watching television, or talking on the phone, and direct your attention to the dog. Say "Outside?" and bring the dog to the backyard. When you are "on alert," you are sensitive to the slightest indication that your dog needs to eliminate. After the dog wets or poops, return to your cooking, continue watching the television show, or call your friend.

To "anticipate" indicates a readiness and an acceptance on your part to take the action that is required immediately—not after you finish reading the mail or sorting the laundry, but right now, this very moment, no matter what. Turn the burner off under the soup so it does not boil over, and take the dog outside now. If you wait, you might be too late.

5 | **Habit Forming Tip:** Don't wait; anticipate. If you think your dog needs to eliminate, take him out right away, or you may be too late.

STEP 4: PUT OUT THE WELCOME MAT

Actively promote one area for piles and puddles. Dogs cannot be expected to intuitively know where you want them to eliminate. However, if you follow four rules, you can create a toilet area that dogs will return to again and again. (Chapter 3 explains in detail how to teach dogs to use a specific toilet area in your yard or house.)

Rule #1. Designate a doggy toilet area that is not near the dog's food, sleeping, or play area.

Rule #2. Place a post or vertical object, even a bucket, to encourage a male dog to lift his leg in the designated toilet area.

Rule #3. Keep the toilet area clean so the dog will not look for a "less crowded" location. Dogs tend to return to the same place to eliminate. However, to attract their attention to your designated doggy toilet area allow one pile to remain there.

Rule #4. Use praise, food, toys, balls, and games to show a dog that puddles and piles in the right location are welcome events. Don't make a dog afraid of you by yelling, screaming, or shouting. Instead, teach your dog that when he eliminates in the target area, he earns rewards.

Whenever the Dog Goes, There You Are

The best comment I ever heard was from an elderly client who said, "My dog's life is like my life." Eileen wakes up, her beagle wakes up. They eat breakfast in the kitchen together. Then while Eileen freshens up, Strawberry goes outside for her morning bathroom break. Strawberry lies at Eileen's feet while Eileen reads, crochets, or watches television. They eat lunch together. Every afternoon they walk to the mailbox.

The two of them live together quite comfortably now, but in the beginning the friction between the two of them could have, if fanned, started a four-alarm fire. Strawberry was not just any beagle, but an I'm-from-the-shelter-and-I-don't-need-anyone beagle. When I met them Strawberry was two years old and had lived with Eileen for one week.

Our first discussion centered on whether Strawberry wet on the carpet because she was raised on indoor/outdoor carpeting, or because no one had taken the time to teach Strawberry the house rules. We finally decided that Strawberry preferred carpet. This was an important discovery, because if we limited Strawberry's access to carpeting during housetraining, we could have a better chance for success. And it worked. We kept Strawberry in rooms with tile and linoleum until we had confidence that she would only eliminate on the desert dirt and grass areas behind Eileen's house.

I explained to Eileen that in order to teach this independent, rowdy, two-year-old beagle, we would need to work with the whole dog; not just the back half, but the front half too. Many people dread housetraining dogs. I don't. That's because I've learned a secret. Housetraining goes quicker and dogs learn faster when you work on more than housetraining. In addition to learning the house rules, Strawberry learned to walk on a leash, come, sit, down, sit up and beg, and roll over.

Eileen kept one eye on the dog and her other eye on the clock in housetraining Strawberry. Eileen recognized that 15 minutes or a half hour meant the difference between a successful trip outside or a missed opportunity that resulted in a puddle on the floor. For two weeks, Eileen honed her "sticking power." Sticking power is the ability to face any situation, take responsibility, and follow through until successful. Sticking power combines your ability to teach with the dog's ability to learn. All dogs can learn with enough contact; or, as I like to say, "Whenever the dog goes, there you are."

6 | **Habit Forming Tip:** Housetraining requires teamwork. The dog's output depends on *your* input.

Start Today

It's much easier to change a new behavior than a habit. Habits are acquired through constant repetition, but they start with a single action. For example, Red Sun Rising, my golden retriever, is sent outside to eliminate every night after he eats dinner. Without any prompting, as soon as Red finishes eating, he walks to the sliding glass doors so that I can let him out. Behaviors that continually reoccur become so well established that they occur automatically. Once bad habits are ingrained, it takes longer to change them. There is a huge difference between housetraining a four-*month*-old Great Dane and a four-*year*-old Great Dane.

Luckily for us, a dog's behavior changes before he eliminates. A dog might circle, sniff, become active suddenly, stop and look distracted, wait by the door, pant, whine, act restless, stare, or head toward an area where he has previously eliminated. By paying close attention you will see the signs that tell you to take your dog to the doggy toilet area now!

To make it easy on yourself, follow a schedule and keep a record of when the dog eats, drinks, plays, naps, pees, and poops. In order to figure out the pattern, I like to post a "Doggy Diary" on the refrigerator so I can keep track of my dog's puddles and piles. Then when I plan my timetable for housetraining, I can base it on the dog's natural cycle. If your dog has an accident, write down what you were doing when it happened, such as talking on the phone, watching television, working on the computer, cooking, cleaning, or other tasks.

The Doggy Diary is one of your most important teaching tools. The information you record now gives you the ability to plan a housetraining program that maximizes your time and minimizes your efforts. With the knowledge you gain, you can maintain control of the housetraining process from beginning to end.

DOGGY DIARY: WEEK 1

Day 1 Time/Result/Reward	Day 2 Time/Result/Reward	Day 3 Time/Result/Reward	Day 4 Time/Result/Reward	Day 5 Time/Result/Reward	Day 6 Time/Result/Reward	Day 7 Time/Result/Reward
— — —	— — —	— — —	— — —	— — —	— — —	— — —
— — —	— — —	— — —	— — —	— — —	— — —	— — —
— — —	— — —	— — —	— — —	— — —	— — —	— — —
— — —	— — —	— — —	— — —	— — —	— — —	— — —
— — —	— — —	— — —	— — —	— — —	— — —	— — —
— — —	— — —	— — —	— — —	— — —	— — —	— — —
— — —	— — —	— — —	— — —	— — —	— — —	— — —
— — —	— — —	— — —	— — —	— — —	— — —	— — —
Accidents	Accidents	Accidents	Accidents	Accidents	Accidents	Accidents
Time	Time	Time	Time	Time	Time	Time
What You Were Doing	What You Were Doing	What You Were Doing	What You Were Doing	What You Were Doing	What You Were Doing	What You Were Doing

Symbols: W = wet, P = poop, Ø = no response, ⁑ = reward

DOGGY DIARY: WEEK 2

Day 8 Time/Result/Reward	Day 9 Time/Result/Reward	Day 10 Time/Result/Reward	Day 11 Time/Result/Reward	Day 12 Time/Result/Reward	Day 13 Time/Result/Reward	Day 14 Time/Result/Reward
—	—	—	—	—	—	—
—	—	—	—	—	—	—
—	—	—	—	—	—	—
—	—	—	—	—	—	—
—	—	—	—	—	—	—
—	—	—	—	—	—	—
—	—	—	—	—	—	—
—	—	—	—	—	—	—
Accidents	Accidents	Accidents	Accidents	Accidents	Accidents	Accidents
	Time	Time	Time	Time	Time	Time
What You Were Doing	What You Were Doing	What You Were Doing	What You Were Doing	What You Were Doing	What You Were Doing	What You Were Doing

Symbols: W = wet, P = poop, Ø = no response, ⁂ = reward

CHAPTER 2

• • • • • • • • •

Gain More Time to Train

The best minutes are the pre-planned, padded, extra ones we set aside that come to our rescue when sudden or unforeseen obligations such as rush jobs at work; out-of-state travel; family commitments; or trips to the mall, grocery store, and gas station prevent us from working with our dogs. Fifteen minutes saved by finding a more efficient way of doing things, one hour gained using a schedule based on a dog's natural cycle, or two days rescued when we find assistants to aid us in the training process—these padded minutes help us when we are overtime and out of time, yet still need time to housetrain.

We gain time when we pay attention to our dog's elimination habits and plan our housetraining schedule around her natural cycle. Schedules make time because we don't waste time waiting. We know the best time to take the dog out for a walk or to the paper pads. And we follow the schedule faithfully.

By creating a routine, we arrange time in our favor. Before long, the routine turns into a ritual. Rituals are not always intricate ceremonies with lights, candles, and elaborate costumes;

they are also formalized customs, procedures, and behaviors that work for us so well that we repeat them. One of the rituals in my house is the "after you eat you must potty" ritual. Immediately after Red Sun Rising, my golden retriever, finishes eating, I say "Red. Outside. Tinkletime. Let's tinkle." Red knows the routine. His body expects it; Red anticipates it and goes outside to pee. This ritual not only saves time, it gives me more time, and allows me to praise my dog. Plus, it only takes a minute or less. Sixty seconds. Not bad.

With practice, private rituals evolve into public displays. When Red and I travel to a dog show I say, "Red, tinkletime. Go tinkle." And Red relieves himself *before* we enter the ring. This is a very important routine, since handlers are disqualified if their dogs eliminate inside a ring. However, public displays don't just happen at a show ground. Anytime you take a trip, visit a friend, or walk in a park, you ask the dog for a public display of a private routine that the dog has learned at home.

Schedules that create routines that turn into rituals compound our time. Dogs who know that a walk, game, treat, or toy happens after they eliminate do not postpone, delay, or dawdle; they hurry to earn their reward. Dogs who learn that confinement in a crate, an exercise-pen or x-pen, or room follows their quick elimination often take longer and longer before they eliminate to put off the final trip to the house. Every minute that your dog delays decreases the amount of time available for the rest of your day. To avoid wasting time or unnecessary effort, teach your dog that the quicker he eliminates, the faster he earns his favorite reward. In order to focus your dog's attention on elimination, teach him the difference between a walk and a bathroom break.

HOW TO TEACH LUCKY THE LABRADOR THAT A BATHROOM BREAK IS NOT A WALK

The key to efficient housetraining is to focus Lucky's attention on elimination. By targeting a specific toilet area, you can make it clear to Lucky that a bathroom break is not a walk. On the way to the designated doggy toilet area, do not allow Lucky to sniff, explore, or examine every bush, tree, or flower. Instead, walk quickly to the designated toilet area. Then, stand and wait quietly while Lucky searches for the perfect location for a puddle or pile. After Lucky eliminates, a walk in the park or around the neighborhood is his reward. Dogs eliminate quickly when they realize that the sooner they eliminate, the faster they get to explore the new flowerbeds in the park or the fire hydrant down the block, or visit their favorite streetside vendor.

Do not distract your dog. Hide the food, toy, or ball in a pocket while the dog eliminates.

Take Aim with Time

In 14 days you can teach your dog where and when to eliminate. The secret is to direct, not scatter, your efforts. Like arrows hitting a bull's-eye, four steps improve your use of time and increase the time available for training.

STEP 1: MULTIPLY YOURSELF— FIND SOMEONE TO HELP YOU

Josey and Gretchen live together. Josey goes to college and works part-time. Gretchen is in the last year of her residency at a large teaching hospital in Tucson. Their long-haired dachshund, Roscoe, is seven months old. Luckily, Josey's dad, Bill, lives five minutes away and loves Roscoe. In the beginning, Bill came twice a day to let Roscoe out, exercise him, and play with him. Now Bill visits Roscoe once a day.

Not everyone has a family member or a friend who is willing to visit and care for their dogs. If you don't, look for a pet-sitter or dog walker to help you out with young puppies, adolescent dogs, and dogs who need retraining. Housetraining dogs takes personal attention. There's no way around it. If you cannot spare the time, find someone to help you.

7 | **Habit Forming Tip:** Like arrows hitting a bull's-eye, take aim with your time, and you will have time to train.

STEP 2: PRACTICE TIME PADDING— LEAVE EXTRA TIME

My next dog is going to be named Murphy. Murphy's Law— anything that can go wrong, will go wrong—was probably first spoken by a person who was married with three children, worked full-time, and had to housetrain a puppy.

There are always more demands for your time than is available, but time padding can change your outlook from harried and frantic to willing and able. All you have to do is add extra minutes to the length of time you think something will take. For example, when you take the puppy outside to pee, you *hope* it will only take five minutes, but it's better to plan on the puppy needing 15 minutes. Or, your plan is to walk the dog for 15 minutes in the morning. At the end of your walk, just as you arrive at your door, your neighbor Alice walks up and starts griping about the landlord. Ten minutes later you extricate yourself. Great. Now you have less time to shower and eat breakfast. However, if you padded your dog walking time, you can still talk to Alice and take a leisurely shower.

Time padding changes your outlook and the results of your dog training. You need to figure out the amount of time required if everything goes smoothly. Then estimate how much time you will need if you are interrupted or the unexpected happens. For example, on rainy days, if your dog refuses to walk outside, scheduling an extra 15 minutes will allow you to grab your raincoat, find your umbrella, put the rain boots on the dog, and not be late for work. If nothing happens to interrupt your schedule, you have extra time! If something goes wrong, you have time to deal with the situation. With time padding, time is always available.

STEP 3: IDENTIFY TIME BANDITS—BE AWARE OF WHAT OR WHO STEALS YOUR TIME

Time bandits are interruptions, distractions, and personal actions that cause you to lose your focus and squander your time. They steal valuable seconds, minutes, and hours and handicap your ability to housetrain your dog. Time bandits run off with your time before you realize what happened.

Interruptions are time bandits that undermine your best intentions to school your dog. For example, you come home from work and answer the telephone before letting the dog out. After a 20-minute conversation, you open the door to the laundry room to take the dog outside, but it's too late. The dog could not wait and there is a fresh pile on the floor. Children are expert time bandits. They seem to have an unerring ability to disturb you at critical moments. However, careful planning that uses naptimes, videos, baby-sitters, and games can create the time you need for housetraining. Controlling interruptions requires that you recognize what they are—bandits that cause you to spend your time in unproductive ways.

Distractions hinder your efforts when you steal time from one activity to do something else. It can be as simple as taking your eyes off the puppy while you dig out the bag of potato chips buried under the crackers in the cupboard. Chips in hand, you turn around and spy a new wet spot on the kitchen floor. You

NICE WAYS TO SAY NO TO PEOPLE, AND YES TO YOUR DOG

1. Don't answer the phone. Let your voice mail, answering machine, or caller ID service screen incoming telephone calls.
2. Immediately inform people of your priorities. For example, "I would love to visit with you later, but right now I need to take my dog on a walk."
3. Use conversation stoppers to set time limits such as, "Is there anything else we need to discuss before I leave?"

lost your focus and missed an important teaching opportunity. Distractions such as a noisy dishwasher or loud music hinder your ability to concentrate. However, distractions are easy to control. For example, ask your children to use headsets when listening to music, or run the dishwasher at night.

The wiliest time bandit is not your Aunt Sally, bag of chips, or ringing phone; it's you. Don't steal from yourself. Time bandits lurk in the most innocent places: sleeping in an extra 20 minutes, watching one more television show, or chatting with neighbors instead of schooling the dog. However, you can take control of your time by identifying what you do that interferes with housetraining. In the same way that Michael Jordan focuses on a basketball in center court, know that when it comes to time, the ball is in your hands, and you control whether you dribble, spin, pass, or shoot.

8 | **Habit Forming Tip:** Two seconds or ten minutes spent wisely can add hours to your day.

⏱ STEP 4: IDENTIFY PRIORITIES—DO THE MOST IMPORTANT THING FIRST

Go ahead. Make a decision. However, before you dive into an empty swimming pool, you'd better figure out your priorities. Priorities serve the same function as swimming instructors. They point you in the right direction, keep you up and floating, and help you stay out of trouble by making good decisions.

To define your priorities, you must determine what is most important to the dog's schooling, putting the dog's needs first. The challenge comes as you sort out the difference between what you *want* and what the dog *needs,* and then base your actions on your decision. Look ahead! Determine the consequences of your conduct. For example, you like sleeping until noon on the weekends. However, since you live in an apart-

---

⏱ DO I ANSWER THE PHONE WHEN I AM TRAINING THE DOG? THE ABCS OF DETERMINING PRIORITIES

We often get sidetracked when the phone rings, the clothes dryer turns off, or our teenager cannot find the car keys. We cannot decide if we should clean the bathroom or train the dog. How can you determine what is important and what can be ignored until a later time? Just remember your ABCs. Look at every event and classify it as an A, B, or C.

A = Act now. This event is significant and essential. If it is not attended to immediately, serious problems will result.

B = Bide your time. This event is important, but does not require immediate attention. If the response is delayed, no harm results.

C = Cancel any response. The event is unimportant. If it is not done, no one cares.

ment, the only way your dog can access his toilet area is if you take him outside. If your priority is to have a housetrained dog, you must take him out early in the morning if you want to keep your house puddle- and pile-free. Otherwise, if you do not let the dog out and he poops in the kitchen, how will that affect future housetraining?

 Remember, priorities are like promises. They only work if you honor them.

Give Yourself the Gift of Time

My friend Ann is a great time manager. I love listening to her tell me how she created more time in her schedule when she involved her 10-year-old twin daughters in the housetraining process by explaining that 10 trips outside with their 8-week-old cocker spaniel earned them one visit to the mall, and 15 bathroom trips obtained one visit to the movies. She swears the dog never had an accident. The dog couldn't; he didn't have a chance. The girls had him outside at every opportunity.

Effective time managers like Ann use their time wisely and do not waste it. Ann needed help and knew that her daughters demonstrated the characteristics of effective doggy toilet trainers: patience, watchfulness, consistency, resourcefulness, and happiness.

THE FIRST CHARACTERISTIC: PATIENCE

It's hard to be patient when there are meals to cook, cars to repair, lawns to mow, or laundry to wash. There's not a spare minute, let alone 10 extra minutes, to wait for a puppy to pee as we hurry from weeding the garden to repairing a bicycle tire. We expect puppies and dogs to follow our beat, forgetting that their bodies pulse to a different rhythm. Patient people understand that dogs follow a natural order that has a beginning, middle, and end. It cannot be rushed. Accept it. Use this opportunity to watch the clouds, sniff a flower, or smell freshly mowed grass. Enjoy your time outside.

Jack, who successfully papertrained his papillon in 14 days, used his time waiting for Jubilee to eliminate as a chance to practice his isometrics. He's convinced his chest and arm muscles got stronger by their regular workout during the housetraining period. Jack learned that patience is not an endurance event, but an opportunity waiting to be filled.

THE SECOND CHARACTERISTIC: WATCHFULNESS

In her third-floor Manhattan walkup, Robin lives by the belief that the early bird catches the worm. No signal is too small to escape her observant eyes. Is the sheltie's nose down? Tail up? Are the front paws scratching at the carpet? When she observes Fancy sniffing and circling, the word "Outside?!" tumbles from her lips before Fancy has time to squat and wet. When Fancy runs to the door, Robin praises her at the door because Fancy recognized the word "outside" as a signal that redirects her behavior. Robin never waits until after Fancy eliminates outside, but rewards Fancy for each step along the way, not just the final result.

Robin does more than focus on puddles or piles. She pays attention to the whole process, from what Fancy eats to when she wakes up from a nap, in order to schedule a potty time that fits Fancy's cycle.

9 | **Habit Forming Tip:** Working with dogs is like using a compass; you must take frequent sightings to keep them headed in the right direction.

THE THIRD CHARACTERISTIC: CONSISTENCY

Mac is a mastiff, 145 pounds of lovable canine. However, Mac is 14 months old and in his third home. Mac's first home lasted for six months. The landlord "evicted" Mac from the second-floor efficiency apartment because Mac was over the 35-pound weight limit. His second home was a crowded rescue shelter. His third home was my client Michael's suburban house. Michael had always wanted a big dog and now he had Mac. There was just one problem. Mac wasn't housetrained.

Teaching Mac not to soil in the house tested Michael's commitment. Once is not enough. Learning requires many repetitions before it takes hold. Consistency is more than the ability to hold things together; it is the steadfast adherence to designing a housetraining plan and following it through, no matter what happens.

When Michael accepted the responsibility of housetraining an older dog, he also added the role of parent. In the same way that parents encourage their daughter's first faltering steps by holding her hands, praising her, and walking with her, Michael had to continually guide and reward Mac's behavior. Michael's goal was to reward Mac every time he eliminated in the correct location. And it worked. Michael's system of "first time, every time" developed a completely housetrained dog in 14 days.

THE FOURTH CHARACTERISTIC: RESOURCEFULNESS

Lance is a 4½-month-old Samoyed, a fluffy, white bundle of fur who loves other dogs, children, and the retired, elderly couple who lives with him. There is only one thing that Lance likes better than eating, and that is sleeping. However, housetraining Lance has been a challenge for Bob and Dorothy. They spent three weeks trying to housetrain him with no apparent results. Lance left puddles in the living room and piles in the bedrooms. Bob and Dorothy had tried all the old ways of training dogs such as rubbing Lance's nose in a pile or saying "bad dog" without any success. After they found three puddles in one morning, they called me.

I explained to Bob and Dorothy that resourceful dog handlers continually search for new and better ways to housetrain. Two words—"what if?"—describe how creative people think. For example, when I asked them about their feeding schedule, Bob and Dorothy explained that they always kept dog food in Lance's bowl, so Lance would not get hungry. However, once I described that if Bob and Dorothy controlled when Lance ate, they would have better control over when Lance eliminated, they agreed to establish a feeding schedule. Finding new housetraining solutions was easy after they started asking questions such as, "What if we feed Lance before we bring him outside? What if we take up Lance's water dish before we go to bed? What if we confine Lance to a crate or x-pen if we cannot watch him? What if we don't give Lance free run of the house at night?"

> **Resourceful dog handlers realize they cannot force dogs to eliminate, so they experiment with different approaches until they find ones that work.**

THE FIFTH CHARACTERISTIC: HAPPINESS

Annabelle Lee is a bouncing, excitable, lively Weimaraner whose idea of a good time is to leap over couches and chairs in a crazy "welcome home" dance, fly through the air after Frisbees and balls, and sleep on the bed when no one is watching. Today, Annabelle Lee is a happy dog. However, she was not always carefree. Her previous home was filled with loud voices, harsh words, tossed cans, and slaps with hands or rolled-up newspapers.

Who likes a grouch? Not me. Not your dog. Rough methods turn canine minds off, not on. Luckily for Annabelle Lee, she joined a new family. Craig and Meredith think that dogs are the perfect playmates. They take Annabelle Lee to the park for walks, praise her when she sits or lies down, and give her food treats every time she comes. Annabelle loves to work for Craig and Meredith. Their smiles and happy presence make her schooling sessions seem like playtime. Because dogs want to share the fun and excitement, cheerful people spur dogs to try harder. The best part is Annabelle has never had an accident. Not one.

 Dogs love to work for happy people who use positive rewards that whet their appetite for more schooling sessions. Dogs want to please, not disappoint us.

 FOUR FACTORS THAT AFFECT HOUSETRAINING

1. Dog's environment.
2. Amount of time handler works with a dog.
3. Consistency or follow through.
4. How long the problem has existed.

CHAPTER 3

. . . .

How to Pick the Right Solution: Housetraining vs. Papertraining

Scott had found the perfect place to live. It was a fourth-floor loft in a converted warehouse in Minneapolis. Scott could have lived on the second floor but he chose the fourth-floor loft because it had a spiral staircase that led to a hidden study and an exit door to the roof.

Scott wanted access to the roof since he lived with his sharpei, Andre. Now, Scott could avoid walking up and down the open, metal and concrete stairs five times a day for Andre's walks. The rooftop was surrounded by a five-foot cyclone fence; narrow walkways meandered through open spaces, gardens, and rooftop ventilators. During the spring, summer, and fall, Andre could easily find a place to do his business, but when blowing snow and three-foot drifts restricted Andre's access to the roof, Scott needed another option. After Scott moved in, he built a wooden, four-foot-square doggy litter box, lined it with plastic, filled it with gravel, and placed it next to the door to the roof.

Deciding whether you should housetrain or papertrain your dog is like cutting waist-length hair to above the ears. The decision is not irrevocable, but once you make it, it takes a lot of time and

The perfect environment—litter box, doggy bed, crate, water, tile floor, and gate.

effort to grow a different response. There are significant differences between papertraining and housetraining. Papertraining is *not* the first step before dogs use the out-of-doors for their toilet area. Instead, papertraining creates an *inside* doggy toilet area for the dog to use at all times. Housetraining requires dogs to consistently eliminate outside and never eliminate inside. Choosing between housetraining and papertraining is like approaching a fork in the road. Either way is correct, but your experiences will be very different depending on which route you choose.

The First Decision

Picking the right approach is easy. First, decide whether you want your dog to eliminate inside, otherwise known as perma-

PAPERTRAINING ADVANTAGES

No waiting for elevators.
No walking up and down stairs.
No worrying about contagious diseases.
Toilet area always available.

PAPERTRAINING DISADVANTAGES

Toilet area takes up space.
Toilet area must be cleaned a minimum of once a day, preferably after every use.
Dogs may soil in places other than the doggy toilet area.
Male dogs may mark furniture or walls in their search for a vertical surface.
Big dogs leave large puddles and piles.

HOUSETRAINING ADVANTAGES

No odor or smell inside the house.
More floor space without an indoor doggy toilet area.
City dogs see new sights, people, and places every day.
Suburban or country dogs have easy access to toilet areas.
Easier cleanup.

HOUSETRAINING DISADVANTAGES

Puppies may have some accidents inside the house until they develop bladder and sphincter control.
Waiting for elevators.
Walking up and down stairs.
Standing outside when it's hot, cold, or rainy.
Limited access to grassy toilet areas for city dogs.

nent papertraining, or if you want your dog to eliminate outside. That's it! Inside or outside?

The advantage to inside dogs can be summed up in two words: convenience and safety. A dog always has access to a toilet area; you do not have to worry about rain, sleet, snow, or heat. In addition, you eliminate any anxiety that your dog will meet aggressive dogs or risk exposure to a contagious disease.

The disadvantages to permanent papertraining are that inside dog areas smell, occupy valuable space, and must be cleaned frequently. Also, the dog may eliminate in other areas inside the house, the dog does not see new places or faces, and big dogs leave large puddles and piles.

The advantages to having dogs eliminate outside can be summed up in three words: clean, spacious, and pleasant. Outside, piles are easy to remove and no odors taint the inside air. In-

Papertraining is possible! Zak uses papers in the condo in Pittsburgh and the house in Carefree, Arizona.

side living areas are not cluttered with doggy toilet stations. Suburban or country dogs have easy access to toilet areas. In addition, city dogs have more opportunities for socialization.

There are two major disadvantages to having dogs eliminate outside:

1. For city dogs, it is more difficult to access outside toilet areas because of stairs, elevators, and bad weather.
2. Puppies may have accidents inside the house until they develop bladder and sphincter control.

Ashley, a suburban dog, uses the backyard as her doggy toilet area.

The Second Decision

As soon as you decide whether your dog will eliminate inside or outside, you are ready to make your second decision. Now it is time to designate a location for the doggy toilet area. For example, which room in the house will you use to confine your dog? What part of the yard should be targeted for the toilet area? Where is the best place for a dog to eliminate if you live in the city?

Choose a convenient location for the doggy toilet area. For example, this doggy door allows access to an outdoor run and a tiled bathroom.

The Third Decision

Be it ever so humble, there's no place like home. A dog den is a dog's home. Dogs like areas where they can feel safe, comfortable, and surrounded by things they love such as toys, balls, and a comfortable rug, mattress, or blanket. With a dog den, you can safely leave your dog while you attend to other matters because dogs don't soil where they live when they have regularly scheduled bathroom breaks.

In the same way that you have a home, dogs need a home, too. A dog den is a commonsense solution that fits easily into any lifestyle. When your lifestyle incorporates your dog's needs, housetraining is a breeze.

Your third decision requires you to figure out what teaching tools or equipment your particular lifestyle requires, such as exercise-pens (x-pens), crates, outdoor runs, doors, gates, litter boxes, or pads.

Confining dogs to a small, specific area is based on the idea that dogs will not soil in their den. Using a crate or x-pen allows you to alternate trips to the doggy toilet area and supervised freedom with seclusion inside a den. The key to using crates or x-pens is to immediately take the dog to the doggy toilet area as soon as he exits his den. Then, reward the dog when he eliminates. Do not immediately confine him. The dog has earned at least one hour of *supervised* free time.

Crate or x-pen training was never meant for long-term confinement, except at night. However, even at night you will need to let a puppy out after four or five hours. During the day, confine your dog only if you plan on taking him out once every hour. If you will not be home for an extended period of time, leave your dog in a small room with papers covering the floor.

> 🐾 **If your dog soils inside the crate, you have left him too long without a break.**

Exercise- or X-Pens

Exercise pens consist of eight panels and one door made out of seven- or nine-gauge wire. The hinged panel construction al-

Zoey rests inside her exercise- or x-pen.

lows you to alter the shape of the x-pen. Because it folds up like an accordion, x-pens are easy to move or store in a closet. In addition, you can combine two pens and have an exercise area for puppies or small dogs. X-pens come in different heights from 24 inches to 48 inches. If you decide to use an x-pen to help you with your housetraining, make sure your dog cannot push it around, jump over it, or knock it over.

CRATES

Crates are usually made out of steel with a tray on the bottom that dogs lie on. I prefer metal crates over plastic kennels, since metal crates collapse and are easier to store and move.

If you plan on buying only one crate and you buy a crate to fit a dog and not your puppy, you could end up with a crate that is

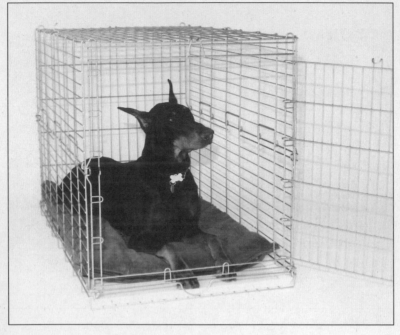

Cody waits inside a wire crate.

so large your puppy could soil in a corner and still have a "clean" den. With a wire crate you can add a wire divider. Then you can decrease the crate's size when the puppy is small and expand it when the puppy grows larger until you can remove the divider completely. Wire crates are easy to clean and allow plenty of air flow, along with a lot of visibility for your dog.

> **Remember, when a crate fits a dog, the dog can easily lie down, stretch out, turn around, and have at least four inches of extra head room when he stands or sits.**

Note. Accessories you might want to add to your crate or plastic kennel are: dog beds, divider panels, and carry carts.

Plastic kennels are required by airlines for transporting dogs. However, if you decide to use a plastic kennel for crate-training be prepared to buy more than one kennel. You cannot add dividers inside a plastic kennel so you will need to buy larger sizes as your puppy grows. Also, check that your dog has enough ventilation inside the kennel, since there are only two small panels to encourage air flow.

Red lounges next to his kennel.

FOUR STEPS FOR INTRODUCING DOGS TO CRATES

Crates were never intended to be all-day storage units. They are temporary training tools. Do not leave your dog in a crate for longer than one hour without a break. Always check that the crate is in a location that allows plenty of air, avoids any drafts, and does not sit in the direct sun. Follow these steps and your dog's introduction to the crate will go smoothly.

Step 1. *Take your time.* Introduce your dog to the crate gradually. Place the crate in a room where you spend a lot of time. Prop the door open so that it cannot swing shut accidentally and bang into the dog. Let the dog look at it and sniff it on his own.

Step 2. *Create a safe and happy "home."* Place a bed and some special toys and bones inside the crate.

Step 3. *Make the teaching sessions fun.* Most dogs walk right in if you throw a favorite toy, bone, or treat inside the crate. Say "Crate!" and toss a treat. Another method is to call the dog's name, say "Crate!" and wiggle a treat through the wire mesh at the opposite end of the crate. *Do not close the door!* Ask the dog to enter his crate several times a day. When the dog goes inside, reward him.

Step 4. *Short schooling sessions build a dog's confidence.* Once the dog willingly walks inside the crate, close the door. *Do not lock the door!* Sit quietly next to the crate. After 15 seconds open the door. However, encourage the dog to stay inside the crate by having toys and bones to distract him. Increase the amount of time the door is closed.

Now you can fasten the crate's door. After you lock the door, stay quietly next to the crate. After three minutes, release the door. Continue to increase the time the dog is inside the locked crate. Once the dog rests quietly inside the crate, you can move around or leave the room.

 Note. Use this same process for introducing dogs to x-pens.

Outdoor Runs

Outdoor runs are usually made out of chain link fencing. They can be any size or shape. Important considerations with an outdoor run are that the dog is protected from the elements, has plenty of shade, and has a comfortable place to lie down. Flooring choices include grass, tanbark, dirt, cement, rubber matting, or gravel. Roofs can be metal, vinyl, wood, or plastic to protect the dog from the elements. The best use of an outdoor run is to attach it to the house so that the dog can walk through a doggy door to enter it.

Dogs who are *permanently* kept in runs do not have the same learning opportunities as dogs who live inside and use runs as dens. Outside dogs have no one to teach them correct or incorrect places for eliminating. Without any instruction, when outside dogs enter a house, they might soil in it because the house is not their "home." Even if you expect your dog to live outside, begin his housetraining inside. Then, if your dog ever comes inside, he will know the house rules.

Luke relaxes inside his outdoor run.

Doggy Doors

Doggy doors are two-way portals that use magnetic weather-seal doors, sensor collars, or flexible flaps to provide 24-hour entry to toilet areas. A doggy door placed in an inside wall or door allows easy access to a storage or laundry room where puppy papers are hidden. A doggy door fitted to an outside wall or door gives a dog a permanent entrance to the backyard or outdoor

10 | **Habit Forming Tip:** If you watch and praise your dog at least once a day when she uses the doggy door to eliminate outside, you will maintain good doggy manners.

Stutz uses his doggy door.

run. People who rely on doggy doors must still teach their dogs to notify them when they need to go outside in case the doggy door is ever closed.

GATES

Gates come in sizes that range from door-size to room-size. Gates expand to fit your needs; longer gates contain doors, smaller gates often have one-hand releases. I prefer metal or wire mesh gates, since most dogs do not chew them. All gates should be firmly attached to walls with screws. However, nonskid

Ashley stays behind the gate.

pads, adjustable fittings, and pressure mountings are additional features that affect fit and function. Spring-loaded gates are good for small dogs or dogs who only need a visual barrier. However, they are often hard to secure so that dogs cannot push them over.

LITTER BOXES AND PADS

Litter boxes and pads designate inside toilet areas. Pads can be anything from newspapers to commercially produced protection pads that lure dogs with a chemically created scent. Large

> **If you need a litter box with short side walls and cannot find one for your teacup poodle, buy a kitty litter box, or cut the walls of a cardboard box to the right size, line it with plastic, and then place litter, sand, or papers on top of it.**

puppies or dogs require that you place two or three pads next to each other in order to create the appropriate size toilet area. If the toilet area is too small, the dog will go to the papers, squat, and miss them. In the beginning, do not remove all the dried puddles or piles. The best way for dogs to return to the same areas is for their noses to lead them to it.

Kate uses the litter box.

Once You Make a Few Decisions . . .

I never had any problems housetraining dogs—not my golden retrievers, clients' Airedales, or friends' Dobermans—once I realized that it takes two oars to row a boat. Housetraining is a team effort. It requires that you develop sensible rules, follow a routine, and take personal responsibility for the outcome. Asking a dog to be housetrained without any input from you is like forcing someone to row a boat with just one oar. You can't do it. Doggy manners are created one stroke at a time with both of you pulling in the same direction. Go ahead. There's a gentle current that's already leading you in the right direction.

PART 2

······································

Get Set!

CHAPTER 4

. . . .

It's a Dog's Life: City, Suburban, and Country Living

Home, for me, has always included dogs whether I lived in a farmhouse in Virginia, a third-floor apartment in Minnesota, or a townhouse in Florida. Without easy access to a fenced-in backyard, my dogs have learned to "hold it" while walking to a rooftop doggy walk, riding in elevators, or running down three flights of stairs. Just like mail carriers, neither rain, sleet, snow, nor heat has prevented my dogs from doing their business in the tall grass, desert dirt, or on a cement curb.

Now that I live in horse country, my dog is "boundary trained." Red Sun Rising could easily jump through the gaps in the three-board fence or climb through the open, four-rail, horse stalls, but he doesn't. He has learned to respect, and not cross, the confines of his turnout area.

City, suburban, and country dogs have the same need to eliminate. The critical issue is how they access their toilet areas; it varies depending on where they live.

City Dogs

City living challenges your commitment and creativity and tests the dog's patience. Even with the best dogs, waiting for an elevator or walking up three flights of stairs complicates housetraining. Housetraining urban dogs requires that you concentrate on three areas that can impact your success or failure: noise, distractions, and location.

NOISE

Cities are noisy places. Car horns honk; police, fire truck, and ambulance sirens scream; jackhammers shatter streets; and pedestrian voices swirl and surge through this steel and cement womb. Dog ears, sensitive enough to hear the soft whoosh of an opening refrigerator door, are pierced by city noises like a hot knife through cold butter. In order for dogs to eliminate, they must be relaxed. If the sound of a siren or the screech of brakes grabs their attention and scares them, it takes much longer for them to do their business.

 ### WHEN MISSY THE AIREDALE GETS SCARED

If Missy becomes frightened, do not pick her up or pet her. You will maintain, not reduce, her fears. The best way to comfort Missy is to return her attention to you. For example, change the situation from upsetting to enjoyable by asking Missy to chase a ball, shake hands, roll over, sit, or lie down. When dogs like Missy change their focus from what's "out there" to paying attention to you, sounds become part of the background. Act happy. Stay calm. If you don't get uptight, neither will your dog.

Expose your dog to city noises during times other than bathroom breaks. Find an outdoor café and have the dog lie at your feet as you drink your caffe latte. Take your dog along while you browse at a newsstand or wander through a flower shop. Open your windows or make a tape of city noises to play inside the house.

Dogs familiar with city noises can ignore them and concentrate on eliminating. In the same way that air rushes through an open window on a windy day, noises can flow past dogs without scaring them. All it takes is the right introduction.

11 | **Habit Forming Tip:** When the unknown becomes the familiar, fears disappear. A proper introduction saves time and prevents problems.

DISTRACTIONS

City distractions wash over us like the churning of a river as it flows over rocks, runs under bridges, and cascades into a glorious waterfall. Truck crews fill potholes, street artists attract crowds, and enticing smells from sidewalk vendors scent the air with spices. Whether it is gum on a sidewalk, four kids playing, or another dog, sights and smells grab a dog's attention. Dog minds, always inquisitive, can lose their focus when activity surrounds them. In order for dogs to eliminate, they must focus. If kids on Rollerblades distract them, it takes much longer for them to eliminate.

> 🐾 To minimize distractions, socialize your dog. Take walks with friends and their children, meet new dogs, visit the park, go to a playground and watch the kids play.

🐕 WHEN TEX THE BOXER GETS STRESSED

When Tex becomes anxious, move farther away from the distraction until he relaxes and no longer notices it. Now ask Tex to play with a toy, perform a sit or down, or do some tricks. After he relaxes, move a little closer to the distraction. At the new location keep Tex's attention focused on you. After a few minutes if Tex ignores the distraction, move closer to it. If Tex shows signs of stress, return to your previous location. Repeat.

It doesn't matter whether you move one foot or six inches at each step. Take your time. Your goal is for Tex to pay attention to you when you are near the distraction. Remember, de-stressing Tex may take more than one session.

> 🐾 Dogs who are acquainted with a city's daily parade of events can concentrate on eliminating in spite of the competition for their attention.

LOCATION

The location of a dog's toilet area in the city is easy as long as you respect the rights of others and follow basic city ordinances. Although you have the right to own a dog, you also have an obligation to clean up after your dog. On-leash dogs need to learn how to potty on cement, asphalt, and the occasional spot of grass.

Frequently, puppies who live in the city must eliminate inside since small bladders cannot wait for you to open the door, lock the door, wait for the elevator, walk through the lobby, and reach the designated doggy toilet area before they relieve themselves. Doggy litter boxes, rooftop gardens, paper pads, and small balconies are areas that can be used so puppies can quickly find relief.

The difference between puppies who relieve themselves inside an apartment and permanent papertraining is one of emphasis and duration. Housetraining centers on teaching puppies to use the out-of-doors as the appropriate place to toilet. All teaching efforts and rewards are linked to an outdoor location.

Stutz "goes potty" on-leash.

However, because an 8-week-old puppy is too young to exert bladder and bowel control, papers or pads cover an *entire* area when the puppy is confined. When the puppy uses the papers she is not praised, scolded, or rewarded. Instead, her behavior is ignored. The papers are used *temporarily* until the puppy is old enough to maintain control.

 Note. Housetraining usually takes longer when puppies use papers inside a house. However, in the case of some puppies, there aren't many options.

WHEN IS A PUPPY OLD ENOUGH FOR BOWEL AND BLADDER CONTROL?

At 3 weeks a puppy starts leaving the den so that he can eliminate where he does not eat or sleep. By 8½ weeks a puppy searches for a particular spot outside the den to eliminate. During this period the puppy needs to eliminate approximately every one to two hours. As the days pass, the time between eliminations increases to every two to four hours until the puppy is about 12 weeks old. The time between eliminations continues to increase until a 6-month-old adolescent dog can wait 8 to 10 hours without eliminating.

Suburban Dogs

Suburban living seems easier, but in reality, it can be much more difficult than living in the city. Doggy doors, baby gates, x-pens, kennels, and crates lull people into a false sense of security. People do not pay as much attention to their dogs because they think that the crate or doggy door will do their training for them. However, dogs who lack supervision often develop bad habits that are difficult to change.

Housetraining suburban dogs requires that you pay special attention to two areas that can impact your success or failure: attention and timing.

ATTENTION

Homes are active places. Phones ring, friends and families visit, children play, and household chores occupy free time. Dogs can easily be forgotten with all the other demands for your attention. When there's no time to train, kennels, crates, and the backyard substitute for careful observation. However, x-pens and doggy doors cannot replace your watchful eyes. Teaching dogs where to eliminate requires that you focus your attention on them, so that the signals they give *before* they eliminate do not pass by unnoticed.

Dogs learn constantly as they explore their environment. If you are too busy to watch and teach them the house rules, they will invent their own. Without guidance dogs follow their instincts, not your desires.

> 🐾 **Devices don't train dogs, people teach dogs. A crate or doggy door cannot replace you.**

 WATCH FOR THESE SIGNS

Circling, sniffing, scratching, whining, sudden restlessness or agitation, running to the door, and returning to a place that the dog has used previously are behaviors that dogs display before they eliminate.

TIMING

The key to successful housetraining requires that the act of wetting or pooping on your verbal signal is instantly linked with a reward. The problem is you don't have five minutes between the puddle and the food treat; you have two or three seconds. Timing is like fans cheering at a basketball game. Players get instant feedback. Fans yell, scream, and cheer when the basketball goes through the hoop, not two minutes later. After two minutes the winner can be the loser. The same is true with dogs. Rewards that happen 10 seconds or two minutes after the behavior occur too late for them to be associated with the deed. However, with timely and effective repetition you can keep your dog on the right track.

12 | **Habit Forming Tip:** Teachers know when, students learn how.

Country Dogs

Country living often has no fences to surround a dog's turnout area. No problem if your dog is boundary-trained; comes when you call; does not chase cows, chickens, elk, sheep, or deer; or lives in an outdoor run. However, open space requires close rapport with your dog and superb listening skills. Housetraining rural dogs requires that you focus on one area that impacts your success or failure: boundary training.

BOUNDARIES

Dirt bikes, cows, cars, coyotes, and stray cats tempt country dogs to leave the security of their yard for a madcap chase down a country lane. Nothing escapes a dog's eyes, ears, and nose; even the air smells different in the country. The best protection is a fully enclosed, dog-proofed yard. However, if that is not possible, boundary training is necessary.

 Boundary training acts like the pull of a magnet on iron filings. Your schooling compels a dog to stay inside the perimeter of your property, even when you are not with him.

Dogs who can balance freedom with limits are safe in any situation. I use boundary training with Red Sun Rising at home and when my husband and I take Red and our horses on a camping trip. When my attention cannot be focused on Red, I send him to the living quarters in the front of the horse trailer. I leave the trailer door open so Red can watch us and have plenty of fresh air, but with my hand I draw an invisible line in front of the door as I say, "Boundary." Red stays inside safely while we set up or break down camp.

Dogs who understand boundaries *learn* self-control. Dogs who respect boundaries *practice* self-control.

HOW TO BOUNDARY TRAIN DOGS

Choose a place where your dog will never be allowed. Start small, for example, with a line that is two to three feet long.

Step 1. Face your dog. Stand quietly.

Step 2. Draw a line on the ground with a stick, dowel rod, or yardstick. As you draw the line, say "Boundary." The dog will have no idea what the word "boundary" means, but dogs usually pause while they try to figure out what we want them to do.

 Note. If you are using a fence as your boundary, touch or tap the fence as you draw the line.

Step 3. Reward the dog with praise and a treat, toy, or ball while he waits.

Step 4. Return to the dog and leave the area with him. After a short play session, return, and repeat steps one and two.

Step 5. Increase the delay between the signal "boundary" and the reward.

Increase the length of the boundary line. *Repeat steps 1–5.*

 Note. Dogs cross boundary lines if you increase the difficulty of the exercise too quickly.

Step 6. Once the dog waits patiently, increase your activity level. Stand across the boundary and hum, sing, jump up and down, wave your arms, sit on the ground, eat a cookie, etc. Do not stare at the dog or call his name.

Step 7. Reward the dog when he respects the boundary. If the dog crosses the line, return him to his area. Say "Boundary" and redraw the line.

Step 8. Return to the dog and leave the area with him. After a short play session, return, and repeat step six.

Step 9. Once your dog respects the boundary when you are on the other side, increase the level of distraction. Ask your friends to come and ride bicycles, bring dogs or children, play ball or Frisbee, anything that might cause your dog to cross the boundary.

 Note: Dogs cross boundary lines if you increase the difficulty of the exercise too quickly.

Step 10. Reward the dog when he respects the boundary. If the dog crosses it, return him to his area. Say "Boundary" and redraw the line.

Step 11. After your dog understands boundaries, increase the length of the boundary. For example, if your first boundary line is three feet long, increase it to six feet, then 12 feet, etc., until you can draw a boundary line around the dog's entire turnout area and he will not cross it.

Step 12. Leave your dog in his turnout area while you watch him from a distance. Then, increase your distance until the dog cannot see you, but you can see him. Reward and repeat.

CHAPTER 5

• • • • • • • • • • •

How Dogs Learn

If you want to know how learning happens, draw a rainbow. Go ahead. Start with a big, fat, purple crayon and draw an arc from the bottom of the paper to the top. Stop. Ask yourself, is it a rainbow? Not yet, but once you add red, green, orange, yellow, blue, and indigo, the rainbow appears. Now draw a pot of gold at the end. If you run out of room, it's okay. Turn over the paper and draw the pot on the other side. There's always room for rewards.

Learning is like drawing rainbows. First, you start with an idea such as, "I want the dog to walk through a doggy door." Now decide what the dog needs to learn in order to perform the behavior. For example, in order to use a doggy door, the dog must walk to the doggy door, push the flap, walk through an opening, and exit outside. Once you figure out the necessary steps, you are ready to teach the dog how to use a doggy door. Remember, learning happens more quickly with the presence of rewards, i.e., the "pot of gold." Determine what will motivate or "color" the dog's experience so that he willingly performs the entire sequence. Keep schooling your dog until the dog understands, i.e., the rainbow appears.

> 🐾 You must link an idea—go outside—to an action—find the doggy door and walk through it—with a response on your part—reward the dog.

What Your Dog Knows

Because dogs cannot write letters or use the telephone to talk, they communicate to each other with physical reminders. Female dogs leave scent signals, pheromones, to inform other dogs they are in heat. Male dogs show their presence or superiority by urinating over or above another dog's mark. Piles claim territory. Fearful dogs urinate submissively to pacify a dominant dog or person. Anxious dogs urinate in response to stress.

Elimination is a natural and normal process that dogs use to mark territories, indicate status, or express tension. Tutoring dogs in the housetraining process requires that you recognize that some behaviors are present at birth while other behaviors result from a dog's interactions with his mother, siblings, other animals, and people. However, we can help dogs learn by using their natural attributes: sight, hearing, taste/smell, movement, and curiosity.

The best dogs are toilet *educated,* not toilet trained. Educated dogs search for information in order to make decisions. For example, puppies look for a paper pad because they have *learned* that wetting on the pad will earn rewards. Dogs ring a bell to indicate they need to go outside, or they listen for voice signals, such as "potty time" or "go spot."

The teaching process is actually quite simple. There are only three ideas to teach your dog:

1. Words are signals.
2. Rewards are wonderful.
3. Correct behavior earns rewards.

THE BUILDING BLOCKS OF LEARNING

L = **Look.** Dogs use their eyes to search out squirrels, cats, and the occasional speeding car, bike, or jogger. Quick movement attracts their attention. What dogs see, they want to know more about. What they want to know more about, they chase. With sight-sensitive dogs, you can use small gestures, change your body position, or use a visual marker, and they will notice it instantly.

E = **Eat.** Dogs are motivated by their sense of smell and their desire for food. If it smells good, it probably tastes delicious. Because dogs like to eat, food rewards are effective teaching tools.

A = **Auditory.** Dogs hear sounds that cannot be picked up by the human ear. What they hear, they focus on. Their acute hearing enables you to use whistles, hand claps, words, and whispers as signals or rewards.

R = **Run.** Dogs are active learners who chase, jump, leap, sniff, dig, and crawl in order to explore their world. Adventure is as close as the nearest candy wrapper, bush, garbage can, or rabbit. Build on their curiosity and stimulate their ability to eliminate quickly by planning an activity or game after they potty.

N = **Natural.** In their search for food, water, friends, mates, and interesting experiences, dogs learn. Dogs develop firsthand knowledge from commonplace and natural situations that occur daily in their environment. Every encounter teaches dogs with or without your presence. Expect it, accept it, and plan for it.

Teachers understand that dogs make choices all the time. For example, the dog decides whether he will lift his leg inside the house or use the doggy door and decorate a tree trunk. Good teachers recognize that they cannot force the dog; the dog controls his own behavior. Teachers want dogs to make the right choice, so they design lessons that clearly show that the correct behavior earns praise, food, toys, bones, treats, or games.

The best teachers anticipate a dog's needs and do not make dogs search for an answer, but have the solution instantly available. For example, they know that puppies normally wet as soon as they wake up after a nap, so they fasten a bell on their collars so that they can hear when the puppy starts to move.

Words as Signals

Words by themselves have no significance until we teach their meaning to our dogs. Although the words "go potty" and "yellow submarine" sound different, even when dogs hear them, they do not understand the idea they express. In order for dogs to understand words, we must associate the words with specific behaviors.

How to Use Signals to Cue Behaviors

The following steps build on a dog's ability to associate a signal with a specific behavior.

Step 1. *Connect a signal with a behavior.* Use a word or sound signal any time the dog offers the behavior. For example, when you see the dog wet say "Go spot, go spot," or emit a short, low, continuous whistle.

Step 2. *Connect a reward with a behavior.* As the dog eliminates, praise him. Reward him with a food treat, playing, or a walk.

Step 3. *Ask the dog for the behavior by using the signal.* Choose a time when Mother Nature is on your side. For example, as soon as your dog gets up in the morning, before you feed him,

🐾 **Do not ask the dog to come to you and then give him a reward. The dog will associate the reward with the act of coming, not eliminating.**

take him outside. Say "Go spot. Go spot." The dog has slept all night and his bladder is full. It will not take very long before the dog relieves himself. The reward you give him will strengthen the association between your request and his response.

🐾 **Rewards not only reinforce a dog for performing a specific behavior, they also solidify your position in the relationship as the leader. They strengthen the relationship between you and your dog.**

Timing

If dog training is the art of understanding, then timing is the skill by which it succeeds or fails. Dogs live in the present, not in the past or the future. Feedback must happen immediately, not six seconds later. Saying, "Good dog!" and praising the dog while she wets or poops acts as a bridge until you can give the dog her treat, toy, or ball. Timing, used properly, links a dog's awareness to the specific act that earned the reward.

Learning Requires Feedback

Melon, a 14-month-old Yorkshire terrier, was a holy terror when Karen first started working with him. Melon barked at her when she scolded him, lifted his leg on her sofa, and left piles under her dining room table.

In the beginning Karen ignored Melon when he left a puddle or a pile in the wrong place. Next Karen tried spraying Melon with water when she saw him lift his leg. When the water didn't have any effect, she changed to perfume. One day Karen slapped Melon after she came home and found a pile on her bed. Now Melon avoided Karen. He cowered under tables and chairs, or ran away when she came home from work. However, she still found little daily "surprises."

Unfortunately for Melon, Karen used two types of feedback—omission and punishment—that usually don't work with house-training problems. Karen thought that if she ignored the problem, it would vanish. It didn't. Without input, dogs do what they want. Then Karen tried punishment, but Melon barked at her. He ignored the water and the perfume. Finally Karen re-sorted to force. However, Karen's slap was not effective because Melon could not link her hitting him in the afternoon to a pile he made in the morning. Instead of teaching Melon that he made a pile in an inappropriate location, Karen taught Melon to fear her. Dogs need feedback to learn, but negative feedback often gives contradictory results. Successful housetraining uses feedback that is positive or gives redirections to stimulate a dog's interest in learning.

Remember, in order for feedback to be success-ful, the dog must associate it with a specific ac-tion. Watch your timing. If more than three seconds elapse between the action and your feedback, the dog will not connect the two events. Dogs are not statues. They quickly change from wetting to running, from pooping to sniffing. If too much time passes between action and reward, you can accidentally reward the wrong behavior.

WHY "NO" DOES NOT TEACH

The word "no" does not redirect a dog's behavior to a better alternative. Although "no" may stop an action, it does not give the dog additional information so that he can make a different choice. Contrast it with the word "outside." "Outside" immediately gives the dog a specific action that contains both a location and a direction.

Five Types of Feedback

Dog training is the art of understanding; that's what makes it challenging. What is obvious to you may not be evident to your dog. What is readily seen by your dog may not be sensed by you. Feedback allows dogs to make choices based upon consequences. The type of feedback you give affects how quickly dogs learn and whether or not a dog will repeat a behavior. There are four types of feedback: omissions, rewards, redirections, and punishments.

#1: OMISSIONS

Doing nothing forces dogs to invent their own answers, and their solutions may not be the same as yours. Behind every problem behavior is a cause. In order to alter a behavior, you need to determine why it happens and what needs to change in order to correct it.

#2: REWARDS

Happy voices, dog biscuits, cheese, squeak toys, balls, friendly rubs, games, and walks show dogs you approve of their behavior. For example, during the first week when your dog eliminates in the proper place, praise him quietly while he wets; walk over and reward him as he finishes. Rewards strengthen performance and increase the likelihood that dogs will repeat the action that earned them rewards. *Positive actions that happen during elimination focus the dog's attention on the behavior that earned the reward.*

Rewards encourage a prompt response. Not only do we want the correct response, we want a prompt response. There is nothing worse than sending a dog outside and waiting while he sniffs, checks out a newly dug squirrel hole, wanders over to inspect the fresh dirt on the garden trowel that you left near the flowerbed, and meanders through the yard. Dogs delay going to the bathroom if, when they finish, they are immediately called back inside the house.

To ensure a prompt response, teach your dog that good things happen after he eliminates. For example, you can throw a Frisbee, play with a ball, go on a walk, give him a bone to chew, or tug on a rope. The possibilities are limitless.

 WHEN TO STOP GIVING REWARDS

Whenever I introduce a dog to a new behavior, I give him a reward every time he performs it. Although I always praise a dog when he eliminates in his toilet area, I reduce the frequency and the intensity of physical rewards such as food and play once the dog consistently eliminates in the target area. After I reward a dog 25 times in a row, I change to a variable schedule of reinforcement. For example, I will reward the dog after the second elimination, the fourth elimination, then the third elimination, etc. However, to keep the dog motivated, I occasionally reward two or three puddles or piles in a row. Then I return to an intermittent schedule. Eventually, I completely eliminate any food rewards. Although I play ball with my golden retriever, I do not play ball with him after *every* toilet time. Dogs, like people, become complacent when they know what will happen next. Just like us, dogs like excitement and surprises, too. Offering rewards at different times keeps dogs eager to perform.

> 🐾 **When activities such as walks, playing Frisbee, or chasing balls are used as rewards, they motivate dogs to eliminate quickly.**

#3: REDIRECTIONS

If you see Chelsea the puppy wetting on the living room carpet, and you say "Outside!" in a loud, low-pitched voice instead of "No," you give her new, important, decision-making information. Although the tone of your voice tells Chelsea that something is wrong, the word "outside" redirects her behavior to a different location. Redirections notify dogs that their current activity is unacceptable and gives them a better alternative.

> **Note.** Remember, the words "outside" and "papers" only have meaning if you have used them previously as a behavior prompt.

> 🐾 **If your dog eliminates in front of you, say "Outside!" or "Papers!" Quietly walk over to the dog. If the dog is small, carry the dog to the toilet area. If the dog is large, walk the dog to the area. Then say "Outside/papers. Go potty." Watch the dog. Reward her if she eliminates. If she does not, bring her back inside and confine her to a crate, x-pen, or laundry room.**

#4: PUNISHMENT

If you yell, hit, squirt with water, or use any other form of negative action, dogs will avoid eliminating in front of you. However, that does not mean they will stop leaving puddles or piles in the house. It just means they will not eliminate in your presence. Dogs learn that if you do not see them, they do not get punished. Dogs associate the hitting or yelling with you, not with their behavior. *Negative actions that happen in conjunction with puddles and piles focus the dog's attention on you, not on the behavior.*

 Punishment that happens after an incident fails to stop housesoiling because dogs do not connect the punishment with a behavior that occurred five minutes or five hours previously.

13 | **Habit Forming Tip:** Don't work harder, work smarter. Create schooling sessions that combine positive feedback and redirections with rewards. You will be amazed at how quickly your dog learns.

Can You Housetrain Your Dog? Yes!

The significant player in the housetraining process is not your dog, it's you.

If you hurry, dogs become anxious.

If you are inconsistent, dogs get confused.

When you establish rules, dogs learn.

When dogs learn, you work together.

Working together, you create the ultimate location—
a happy home.

• • • • • • • • • •

The Three R's: Rules, Responsibilities, and Routine

Housetraining in front of me, where do I start?

Housetraining around me, when does it end?

Housetraining behind me, how to continue?

Good housetraining habits are lifesavers. They keep you afloat even when your cousin and her three children come over for dinner, you are sick in bed with the flu, or you spend the entire weekend writing a report on the computer. Realizing that your briard will tell you if he has to go out, knowing that when you let him outside, he will eliminate "on signal," or recognizing that your Boston terrier uses the doggy door and relieves herself without requiring your presence, decreases the demands on your time.

Teaching dogs the house rules is simple. Dogs already know how to eliminate; you just need to teach them where. Schooling sessions guide a dog's behavior until her response occurs automatically. In the same way that people always turn on the light when they enter a dark room, you want dogs to always go to their toilet area when they need to eliminate.

The teaching process begins when you define the specific habit you desire, such as "The dog notifies me when she needs to go outside." Now you can design lessons that will teach the dog how she can get your attention, such as barking or ringing a

bell. The dog's education is complete when she performs a behavior automatically without your assistance or intervention—for
example, fetching a specific toy and dropping it at your feet to
tell you she needs to go out.

How long housetraining takes depends on you. It's your responsibility, not the dog's. The rules you follow, the routine you
establish, as well as your consistency and vigilance determines
how quickly and easily the dog learns. One of my clients who
works at home *never* experienced a housetraining problem with
her German shepherd. Another client who has a 45-minute
commute to work only needed 10 days and one long weekend to successfully complete her terrier's housetraining. If you
follow the advice in this chapter, your dog will easily learn the
house rules in 14 days or less. However, if you are consistent
and the dog does not improve or the numbers of puddles and
piles increase, visit your veterinarian to make sure the dog is
healthy.

 **If a dog has worms, diarrhea, a urinary tract in-
fection, cystitis, or parasites, it will disrupt his ability to learn potty training.**

 **FIVE COMMON HOUSETRAINING
MISTAKES**

1. Yelling or screaming.
2. Rubbing the dog's nose in a pile.
3. Hitting the dog.
4. Locking the dog out of the house.
5. Spraying the dog's face with perfume, vinegar, or any
   type of repellent.

The First "R": Rules

Every sport has rules. In baseball, it's three strikes and the batter is out; no exceptions. In football, a team must make 10 yards for their first down or possession reverts to the other team; those are the regulations. In the same way that sports maintain a code of rules, housetraining dogs also involves standard methods and procedures. Effective managers recognize that the following six rules facilitate and speed learning.

> 🐾 **Dogs learn best when there are "no surprises."**

RULE #1: START ORGANIZING

Get up earlier, turn off the television, or ask your mother to watch the children for one hour. Your dog needs your undivided attention. One-on-one supervision permits you to give the dog the care she needs. Distractions are confusing for you and your dog. If your attention wanders, you are giving your dog "quantity," not "quality" time. If you want results, you must organize yourself so that you increase, not decrease, your housetraining time.

RULE #2: USE FREQUENT, SHORT SCHOOLING SESSIONS

How long would it take for you to speak Chinese or figure out a new computer software program? Learning to speak Chinese fluently takes years, not days. When I changed from a key-based software program to a mouse-driven program, I attended a special user's seminar, practiced for weeks, and still had to call technical support with questions. Once was not enough.

The key is to practice. Housetraining takes many sessions. Dogs must *live* it. Commands such as "Flash, you will go outside

> 🐾 **Learning takes repetition. In the same way that vitamins taken every day support a healthy body, frequent schooling sessions further housetraining efforts.**

now and wet" are not enough. For the next 14 days, you must consistently link the words "Go potty" to the dog's wetting or pooping, and reward him for his accomplishment. Once Flash identifies the behavior you want, he can do it.

Puppies and dogs give you plenty of opportunities to teach doggy toilet manners. Puppies eliminate at least every one to two hours. In addition, they often wet or poop after they eat, play, or nap. The only exception is at night when puppies sleep. However, during the night most puppies still need a bathroom break every three to four hours. With puppies you can never have too many bathroom breaks.

Adult dogs can usually control their bowels and bladders for eight to 10 hours. However, the length of time that dogs can "hold it" is different from how often they need to eliminate. Dogs always need access to toilet facilities after they wake up, after they eat, and before bedtime. However, exercise, health problems, medications, climate, and availability of food and/or water also affect the number of bathroom breaks they require. For example, if you take your dog out for a three-mile jog and he comes home and drinks a lot of water, you can't expect him to be comfortable "holding it" for eight hours.

14 | **Habit Forming Tip:** Practice makes perfect. The more you practice, the faster the dog learns.

RULE #3: CREATE ELIMINATION OPPORTUNITIES

Like turning on a tap, you can set up situations that produce the results you want. For example, dogs usually urinate more than they defecate. To increase the chance that a puppy might urinate during a specific time period, you can play with a puppy, encourage him to drink water, and then ask him to "Go potty." This increases the likelihood that the puppy will wet. If you pick up a dog's water bowl one hour before his bedtime and confine him during the night, you decrease the likelihood that the dog will need to empty his bladder during the night.

RULE #4: RELAX THE DOG BEFORE "TOILET TIME"

Tense, aroused, stressed, and overactive dogs are more interested in the sights, sounds, and smells around them than in eliminating. In order to relax dogs, I like to run my hands gently over them like a soft breeze to take away any frantic energy that prevents them from paying attention to the task at hand. If you have an uptight canine, finding a way to help her relax means the difference between a short period of time and a lengthy wait for a puddle or pile. You can practice relaxing dogs during grooming sessions, before you leave for the day, or after you return from work. The relaxation sessions can happen in the park, while talking on the phone, listening to music, or watching television. By practicing, the dog will relax more quickly at your touch, before you take her outside.

 Remember, in order to relax your dog, you also need to be calm, quiet, and stress-free.

Zoey relaxes before "potty time."

RULE #5: LINK A BEHAVIOR WITH A REWARD

Rewards are paychecks. How long would you work at your job if you did not earn any money? Dogs, like people, act differently when they get "paid." The most successful dog handlers use positive teaching methods rather than negative correcting techniques. The difference between the two approaches not only affects the speed at which a dog learns where to eliminate, but also affects what your dog thinks, acts, and feels about you.

One of the joys of using rewards—in the form of praise, food, touch, games, walks, toys, or balls—is that a dog wants to participate. He willingly works with you to earn more rewards. Rewards *direct* a dog's attention to his current behavior and *strengthen* the link between his action and the reward. The dog learns his house manners more quickly because both of you are aimed in the same direction.

🐾 **Dogs repeat behaviors that earn rewards.**

Negative correction techniques—squirting vinegar from a bottle; throwing objects such as pillows, keychains, or pop cans; yelling; kicking; or rubbing a nose in a puddle or pile—*redirect* a dog's attention to the handler as punisher and *diminish* the link between a dog's behavior and the correction. This decrease happens whether handlers catch the dog in the act, or if they correct the dog at a later time. The negative correction does not teach the dog that his puddle or pile on the living room carpet was "bad." Instead the dog learns never to eliminate in your presence. Now, housetraining becomes much more difficult, because you cannot teach a dog where to potty if he refuses to eliminate in front of you.

🐾 **Handlers who use negative correction techniques develop dogs who mistrust or fear them, develop shyness problems, hide to potty, and learn more slowly.**

Rule #6: Keep the Doggy Toilet Area Clean

If a dog's toilet area is full of feces or if the puppy's papers are covered with urine, he will look for new places to eliminate. So, clear the air and tidy the space. Start fresh every day and clean up after your dog.

At home, in order to lure a dog back to an outside toilet area, do not pick up all the piles. Leave one pile in the designated toilet area. If you are papertraining, arrange the paper pad into three parts: a plastic bottom layer, a soiled inner layer, and a fresh top layer to lure a dog back to an inside toilet area. Common courtesy demands that if your dog defecates anywhere outside your property, you must pick it up. Always bring a plastic bag when you walk your dog or visit a park.

The Second "R": Responsibility

When Sara was 10, she asked her parents for a dog. She didn't want just any dog, but a purebred Irish wolfhound. However, Sara's parents did not want a dog, let alone an Irish wolfhound that could weigh over 100 pounds. Instead, they bought Sara a Snoopy dog toy for her birthday. Over the next eight years, Sara's parents bought stuffed Garfield cats, killer whales, even an octopus, but no living, breathing, Irish wolfhound entered her life. On Friday evening, that was going to change. After work Sara was picking up her Irish wolfhound puppy, because she no longer lived with her parents. Instead, she lived in a two-bedroom, white frame house across the street from her favorite city park.

On the one-hour drive to the dog breeder, Sara reviewed the items she had bought for her new puppy, Mindy—water dish, food bowl, puppy food, dog collar, leash, dog bed, and baby gate for her kitchen. With every mile that passed, Sara's smile grew wider until her cheeks ached. Her smile changed into a silly grin when she remembered that her vacation started on Monday. Sara would take advantage of the next nine days to keep Mindy company and teach her about life at Sara's house. Sara knew that living with a dog would be so sweet if she could find the time, training tools, and appropriate lessons to teach Mindy about housetraining, and the joys of living with a human pack member.

15 | **Habit Forming Tip:** Be a smart cookie. Use the right ingredients and create a sweet relationship with your dog.

SARA'S RECIPE FOR MINDY

Dough
3 cups love
2 cups fun
1 cup knowledge of dog behavior
1 tbsp good expectations

Filling
2½ cups watchfulness
1 cup listening
½ cup motivation

Mix
Blend, don't beat. Fold in equal parts. Makes one happy, housetrained Irish wolfhound.

Bake for as Long as Possible
Rearrange your schedule. Dogs can't wait.

You Will Need
1 water dish, 1 food bowl, 1 bag puppy food, 1 dog collar, 1 leash, 1 dog bed, and 1 baby gate.

The Third "R": Routine

Dogs like a routine. They like knowing that every morning as soon as they get up, they go outside. They return eagerly after their doggy toilet because they know that breakfast awaits them. Their expectations influence their behavior. A consistent schedule, appropriate food and water, regular exercise, and the presence of a dog den maximize a dog's natural inclination to eliminate at the right time and in the correct location.

SCHEDULE

It does not matter whether it is Monday or Sunday, once you start housetraining your dog, use the same schedule. If you feed your dog at 7:00 A.M. on Monday, feed the dog at 7:00 A.M. on Sunday.

   The only housetraining difference between puppies and adult dogs is the amount of time they can control their bladders. Until puppies are 12 weeks old, they usually urinate every one or two hours during the day and often require a potty break during the night.

   In order to keep puppies on a schedule, you will need to set your alarm clock for a nighttime potty break. However, 3:00 A.M. potty breaks will not last forever! By 12 to 14 weeks puppies should be able to sleep through the night. As the puppy gets older, move the nighttime break an hour later until it occurs at the same time as the morning bathroom break.

KEYS TO CREATING A SUCCESSFUL SCHEDULE FOR PUPPIES, ADOLESCENT, OR ADULT DOGS

- No between-meal snacks. If you control when dogs eat and drink you have a much better chance of determining when they will eliminate.
- Assemble the paper pad into three parts: a plastic bottom layer, a soiled inner layer, and a fresh top layer. Remember, the scent from a soiled inner layer encourages dogs to use the same area.
- If the dog does not eliminate, return him to his den. Then, take him out 30 minutes later.
- Active canines, dogs who have just finished walking or playing, and dogs who live outside always need water. In addition, hot summer temperatures, as well as dogs who live in hot climates, require that a constant supply of water be available.
- Your goal is to always have the puppy or dog eliminate in an appropriate place. The more times you take them out, the less chance there is for an accident.

Adult dogs can control their bladder or bowel for eight to ten hours in the daytime without difficulty. If they eliminate before they go to bed, they do not need a middle of the night potty break. However, dogs who are consistently asked to hold their urine for long periods of time can have problems with urinary tract infections.

The following schedule is a routine that works well for most dogs. I always include a midday walk, eat, water break during the initial housetraining. If you cannot continue it after your dog is housetrained, every two days slide the midday walk an hour later until the "noon" walk coincides with the dinner walk. Remember, puppies need access to an inside toilet area or more potty breaks than adult dogs.

Use a doggy diary so you can plan a schedule that is tailored to your dog's natural rhythms. *Always* alternate periods of confinement with supervised bathroom breaks and free time.

FOOD AND WATER

You are what you eat. How many times have you heard that phrase used in reference to people? Well, the same is true for dogs. Good nutrition affects your dog's health, behavior, and disposition, as well as the size and amount of stools.

What is important for successful housetraining is that your dog eats a high-quality dog food. Follow the general guidelines on the back of the dog food and adapt them to the health, activity level, and lifestyle of your dog. There are many types of dog food. However, any food that is not easily digested can increase the amount of waste eliminated daily, or cause problems such as runny stools, and other health issues.

Dogs have different food and water requirements depending on their age, amount of exercise, where they live, overall activ-

SAMPLE SCHEDULE

Time	Food & Water	Activity	Dogs	Puppies
6:00 A.M.		bathroom break/walk	X	X
6:15	Breakfast		X	X
6:30		bathroom break/walk		X
6:45		Supervised free time	X	X
7:15		bathroom break/walk		X
Confine in a specially prepared room, crate, or x-pen. Puppies need access to an inside toilet area if they cannot have bathroom breaks every hour.				
10:45		bathroom break/walk		X
11:00	Lunch			X
11:15		bathroom break/walk	X	X
Confine in a specially prepared room, crate, or x-pen. Puppies need access to an inside toilet area if they cannot have bathroom breaks every hour.				
4:45 P.M.		bathroom break/walk	X	X
5:00	Dinner		X	X
5:15		bathroom break/walk		X
5:30		Supervised free time	X	X
8:00		bathroom break/walk	X	X
8:15		Supervised free time	X	X
9:30		bathroom break/walk		X
Bedtime	Remove water	bathroom break/walk	X	X
Confine in a specially prepared room, crate, or x-pen.				

ity level, and breed. As a general guideline, puppies have higher protein, fat, vitamin, and mineral requirements, and they need to eat at least three times a day. Working or performance dogs require a higher fat content in their diet. Older dogs need more protein.

16 | **Habit Forming Tip:** Read dog food labels. Search out the best ingredients. Become a knowledgeable consumer.

The climate, as well as whether your dog lives inside or outside, also affects the amount of water he drinks and the type of food he eats. In the summer, dogs need more water. Dogs who live in areas such as the Arizona desert or the Florida subtropics need access to water at all times. In addition, electrolytes or natural coolants like watermelon and apples may be necessary to maintain their internal fluid balance.

At night when I begin the housetraining process, I remove a dog's water dish at bedtime if the dog lives inside. Dogs do not usually drink water during the night because their metabolism slows down when they sleep. However, I never remove the water dish of a high-energy canine, a dog who stays outside, or one who lives in the heat; they require a constant source of fresh water.

🐾 **Do not leave a full bowl of kibble out all day for your dog to eat as he pleases. In order for housetraining to work, you must create a set feeding time. If you do not control when the food goes in, you cannot determine when the food will come out. Always feed the dog in a quiet place where he can eat undisturbed, at the same time every day.**

HOW TO CHANGE A FREE-CHOICE FEEDER TO A PLANNED MEAL PARTNER

Step 1. Determine how much food your dog should eat in one day. If you are uncertain about the appropriate amount, follow the guidelines on the dog food package or ask your veterinarian.

Step 2. Feeding schedule. If you feed the dog twice a day, measure ½ the amount of the total day's dog food. If you feed the dog three times a day, measure ⅓ the amount of the total day's dog food.

Step 3. Call your dog. Set the dog's dish on the floor. Leave the room. After 15 minutes if the dog has not eaten, pick up the food. Do not feed him until the next established mealtime.

Step 4. Practice patience. Wait for two days. As long as your dog drinks water, he can miss a few meals. Remember, hungry dogs eat.

Step 5. Do not feed the dog any between-meal snacks or goodies.

EXERCISE

Exercise can be a brisk walk, playing ball, tossing a Frisbee, jumping, or running. Effective exercise stimulates a dog's cardiovascular system, renews a dog's spirit, and focuses her mind.

Do not confuse taking your dog out to eliminate with exercise. When you target a toilet area with the dog on-leash, walk to a specific area, stand quietly, give the dog a word signal such as "Go potty," and wait for the dog. If your dog's toilet area is in the backyard or on papers inside the house, direct her to it, give the word signal, and wait quietly.

Toilet time is quiet time. You want the dog to concentrate on finding the right spot to eliminate, and it's easier for dogs to pay attention with fewer distractions. The best way to not interrupt a

Many days 11-year-old Chief acts like a puppy. He plays ball with the stiff legs of an old dog, but displays the joy of a 6-month-old.

dog's search for the right location is to keep any movement on your part to a minimum. As you stand quietly and wait in one place, your body posture clearly indicates to the dog that the purpose for this session is a puddle or pile. After your dog eliminates, then you can play games or go on a walk.

17 | **Habit Forming Tip:** Use exercise as a reward for puddles and piles in the right spot. Dogs eliminate more quickly when they know that a walk or a game is their reward.

Standing quietly and waiting brings the best results.

DOGGY DEN

Dogs, like people, like a space they can call home. Doggy dens are shelters, hiding places, and refuges. They are quiet places where dogs go to retreat. Dens offer protection and safety. During the housetraining process, you need a place where a dog can be contained within specific limits or boundaries. Secured, well-fastened, doggy dens are *temporary* measures that enable you to limit a dog's freedom when you cannot watch him. After your dog is completely housetrained and no longer needs to be confined, the doggy or x-pen door stays open so that the dog can come and go at any time.

The crate doors are always open. With seven dogs at home, Harmony and Mercedes use the crates as hideaways when they need some peace and quiet.

🐾 **Control does not mean containment. Control signifies that a dog restrains himself without any intervention on your part. Self-control is an active, not passive, process. The only way a dog can learn self-control is for you to teach him the house rules and give him the freedom to make the right choice, so you can reward him.**

18 **Habit Forming Tip:** It doesn't matter which path you take as long as you always remember to keep to the right, i.e., Be at the right place, at the right time, to get the right response from your dog.

HOW TO CREATE A SECURE AND COMFORTABLE DOGGY DEN

If the den is a kitchen, laundry, or bathroom try this:

1. Use childproof locks on cupboards.
2. Fasten lids on garbage cans.
3. Remove toilet paper roll.
4. Raise towels.
5. Take away small rugs.
6. Remove electrical cords.
7. Use only the strongest materials. For example, screw gates into walls, do not wedge them between walls; and do not buy plastic or wooden gates that are easily chewed and destroyed.
8. Fasten wire mesh in front of gates with wide spaces between bars so that small heads or bodies cannot poke through and get stuck.
9. Spray Bitter Apple® or drip a strong-tasting mouthwash on furniture or objects that cannot be removed to deter dogs from chewing on them. Try a small spot first to make sure it does not stain the wood or fabric.
10. Place papers or the doggy litter box away from the dog's food and the room's entrance.
11. Add toys, Kongs, and Buster Food Cubes for the dog to play with, as well as a doggy bed for naptime.

If the dog's den is a crate or x-pen try this:
1. Check that air flows easily through the den.
2. Evaluate the size of the den; a dog should be able to stand up, turn around, and stretch out with at least four inches of space between his head and the top of the crate.
3. Add a dog bed, rug, Kongs, and bones for the dog to chew.
4. If possible, when you change rooms, move the den to your location so you can listen for any restless or agitated movements that often precede puddles or piles. Place the crate in an area that allows plenty of air, avoids any drafts, and does not sit in the direct sun.

 IS THE DOG READY?

✔ Does the dog respond when you call his name?
✔ Have you taught the dog "Sit" or "Down"?
✔ Does the dog play games with you? Play with toys? Eat treats from your hand?
✔ Have you taught the dog that good behavior is rewarded with treats, toys, or games?
✔ Is the dog leash-trained?
✔ Does the dog understand that words are signals?

ARE YOU READY TO HOUSETRAIN YOUR DOG?

✔ Do you realize that housetraining establishes the tone of your relationship?

✔ Do you understand how dogs learn?

✔ Do you know different ways to reward your dog?

✔ Do you know the difference between redirections and punishment?

✔ Have you learned to link words to specific actions?

✔ Have you lined up other people to help you?

✔ Have you made time in your schedule for housetraining?

✔ Is your teaching time free from other demands and distractions?

✔ Do you know how you will handle accidents?

✔ Do you know who to ask for help if you get frustrated?

✔ Are you aware that puppies cannot physically control their bowels and bladders until they are 12 to 14 weeks old?

✔ Are you aware that a dog's previous experiences affect his current training?

✔ Have you determined if you will papertrain or housetrain?

✔ Do you have the necessary equipment?

PART 3

Go!

CHAPTER 7

• • • • • • • • • •

Getting There Is Half the Fun

Rollerblading stretches your legs; riding a mountain bike pumps your adrenaline; driving a car on winding roads tests your skills; cantering a horse down a sandy wash builds your strength; however, housetraining dogs stretches your mind and exercises your staying power.

When I work with dogs I want to playSMART. Ask yourself, would you rather go to a party or go to work? Easy answer. Let's party! No one wants to work all the time. Not me. Not you. Not your dog. Besides, happy dogs learn faster. All it takes is a little imagination and humor on your part—imagination to figure out the quickest, easiest, and most enjoyable ways to school your dog; and humor to handle the times when in spite of your best efforts things just don't go right. When I playSMART I can balance serious attention to housetraining with playing games, teaching "Sit" or "Down," and practicing tricks; important listening and leadership exercises.

The playSMART approach recognizes that dogs want to have fun, and that dogs learn faster when schooling sessions feel like playtime. A play format uses toys, games, and activities to motivate dogs, teach new behaviors, and eliminate any tension in the learning process.

Red loves to playSMART with balls.

Dogs need three skills in order to keep puddles or piles in the right spot.

Skill #1. Notify someone.
Skill #2. Find a spot.
Skill #3. Use it.

Games That Teach Skills

SKILL #1: NOTIFY SOMEONE

Too amazing. Right now as I am sitting at my computer writing the beginning of this section, Red Sun Rising appears. He walks up, looks at me, turns around, and heads out my office door. He waits, facing the stairs going down. This is Red's signal for me to open our sliding glass doors and let him outside for a potty break. I interrupt my writing and let him outside.

Dogs who notify you when they need to go outside are a joy to live with. It's an easy skill to teach and it starts by playing a game called Find Me!

HOW TO PLAY FIND ME!

Equipment needed: treats, toys, balls

Step 1. Stand at least six feet away from another person who is holding Jo-Jo the Rottweiler. The person holding Jo-Jo says "Find Kate!" and releases the dog.

 Note. Say the name the family normally uses, such as Mom or Aunt Kate.

Step 2. Reward Jo-Jo when she finds you.

Note. If Jo-Jo does not come to you, kneel down, whistle, and show her that you have her favorite treat, ball, or snack.

Step 3. Move farther apart. Repeat steps 1 and 2.

Step 4. Move to a different room than Jo-Jo. The person holding her says "Find Kate!" and releases her.

Step 5. Reward Jo-Jo when she finds you. Repeat in different rooms of the house.

After Jo-Jo consistently finds you anywhere in the house, you can add other family members' names to the Find Me! game. The last step is to teach Jo-Jo that when she finds you, you will take her outside for a potty break.

Step 6. After Jo-Jo finds you, say "Outside?" and let her out. Give her your "Go potty" signal. Praise and reward her when she eliminates.

Note. You will get the best results with this game if you plan your final lesson around the time that Jo-Jo normally needs to go outside.

Just recently one of my clients told me that her daughter Gayle's 6-month-old Australian cattle dog left a pile next to a closed dog door. The dog had not notified Gayle that he needed to go outside because no one had taught him that lesson. Gayle had closed the dog door because the dog had tracked in mud and grass from the wet backyard. Unfortunately, Gayle forgot to open it again. All dogs need to learn the Find Me! game for the times when you are staying in hotels, visiting friends, traveling in a car, or closing the dog door because of rainy weather.

🐾 **Remember, teaching your dog the Find Me! game is just the beginning. Play other games with your dog, such as fetching a ball, catching a Frisbee, puppy-in-the-middle, or searching for the television remote control. You want to be your dog's favorite play partner, as well as the person who gives him access to the out-of-doors.**

SKILL #2: FIND A SPOT

One of the biggest challenges with permanent papertraining is teaching dogs to only use one location in the house as their toilet area. However, you can teach dogs to find their spot by playing the Papers game. Papers teaches dogs how to find their toilet area no matter where they are inside the house.

HOW TO PLAY PAPERS!

Equipment needed: treats

Step 1. Hold Banjo the Chihuahua. Stand two feet away from the dog's indoor toilet area. Say "Papers!" as you toss a dog treat that lands on the *clean* papers. Release the dog. After the dog eats the treat, return the dog to his previous position and throw another treat on the papers.

Step 2. Move four feet away. Repeat step 1.

Step 3. Move farther away. Repeat step 1.

Step 4. Place a treat on the papers. Go with the dog to a different room. Say "Papers!" Release the dog. Repeat in different rooms of the house.

Step 5. After Banjo consistently finds the papers from anywhere in the house, you are ready to give him your "Go potty" signal when he reaches the papers. Praise and reward him when he eliminates.

 Note. You will get the best results with this game if you plan your final lesson around the time that Banjo normally needs to eliminate.

SKILL #3: USE IT!

Dogs who use a designated doggy toilet area without any prompting from you have successfully mastered the first two skills. In order to target a specific toilet area, dogs must learn to listen, pay attention, practice self-control, and offer appropriate behaviors. The same qualities are needed in playing games, executing obedience exercises, and performing tricks. Teaching dogs how to sit or ring a bell is fun. In addition, it builds important listening skills and increases dogs' desires to work with you, which helps your housetraining. Dogs who understand that specific actions earn rewards are motivated to target a specific toilet area to earn attention, praise, food, games, or friendly rubs.

HOW TO TEACH SIT

The sit exercise teaches dogs that a specific behavior earns a reward. Dogs who sit when you say "Sit" have learned that words have meaning. You want dogs to understand the difference between "Sit," "Down," "Outside," and "Go potty now!"

Step 1. Place a food treat, ball, or toy in your hand. Hold it a couple of inches in front of the dog's nose.

Step 2. Slowly raise your hand up and move it toward the dog's hindquarters.

Step 3. When the dog sits, praise and reward.

Step 4. Repeat steps 1–3.

 Note. If the dog doesn't sit, find a better lure. For example, change from a dry biscuit to a small piece of hot dog. Also, check your hand position. If the dog is jumping up, lower your hand. Be patient. The dog will figure it out.

Hold the lure over the dog's head.   *Sunny sits.*

Step 5. Once the dog understands how to sit, then add the word "Sit."

Step 6. Repeat Steps 1–5. Do not move to Step 7 until you have linked the word "Sit" with the resting of the dog's hindquarters on the floor, and a reward, at least 25 times.

 Do not attempt 25 repetitions in one schooling session. Stop before the dog loses his attention and focus.

Step 7. Without a reward in sight, say "Sit." If the dog sits, reward him. If the dog does not sit, repeat the previous steps.

Step 8. End the exercise by saying "Finish" or "Release."

Tricks That Teach

If you want to have fun, teach your dog a few tricks. The dog will like learning them and you will enjoy showing the tricks to friends and family. Tricks also teach dogs that their behavior earns rewards. There are so many tricks—roll over, crawl, walk through my legs, walk backwards, shake, count. Three of my favorite tricks are Rise and Shine, Help! There's a Treat on My Nose, and Ring a Bell. The following five rules will help you develop a successful trickster.

Rule #1. Introduce or practice tricks during your dog's active time, not her naptime.

Rule #2. Do not move on to the next step if the previous step is not reliable.

Rule #3. In order to do tricks it helps if your dog knows basic signals such as sit, stay, wait, as well as "Take it" and "Leave it." (Page 122 explains how to teach "Take it" and "Leave it.")

Rule #4. Capitalize on your dog's natural behaviors and turn them into tricks.

Rule #5. Don't get too serious. Take the pressure off, playSMART and have fun.

RISE AND SHINE

Step 1. Ask the dog to sit. He must be square and balanced with equal weight on his hindquarters, or he will not have the foundation he needs for this trick. (The dog's back should be straight. It should not make an S curve.)

Note. If the dog needs help balancing, put your dog in a corner or against a wall, or stand directly behind the dog with your heels together and your toes pointing out next to his hindquarters; your legs will support his back.

Step 2. Talk to the dog. Keep his attention on you as he waits for the treat.

Step 3. Move the lure up, one inch at a time, over the dog's head.

Trevor rises and rests on his hindquarters when a food lure leads him up.

 Note. Do not move the lure too fast or too high, or the dog will stand up, not rise and shine.

Step 4. Say "Rise and shine" as the dog balances on his hindquarters.

Step 5. Reward the dog.

Step 6. End the trick by saying "Finish" or "Release."

This trick teaches dogs that waiting, listening, and following directions earn rewards.

HELP! THERE'S A TREAT ON MY NOSE!

Kneel in front of small dogs; stand in front of large dogs.

Step 1. Put the dog on a sit-stay.

Step 2. *Gently* hold the dog's muzzle.

Step 3. Place the treat on top of the dog's nose. Always use the same size treats and put them on the same spot on the dog's nose. Use one finger to hold the treat in place. A good spot to put the treat is right behind the dog's nose.

Terry balances a ball on Sunny's nose.

Note. Talk to the dog. Keep his attention focused on you.

Step 4. Say "Easy, easy." You want the dog to slow down in order to have enough control to catch the treat, so draw out the word "EEEEasy."

Sunny waits.

 Note. In the beginning the dog's head will snap and the treat may fly through the air. It takes dogs a few lessons to figure out how to move their muzzle so that the treat doesn't fly off across the room.

Step 5. Release your fingers. Say "Help yourself!"

This trick teaches dogs that lesson time is one more way to have fun.

Sunny catches the ball.

RING A BELL—IT'S POTTY TIME!

Step 1. Tie a string on a bell.

Step 2. Attach the bell to a doorknob with the string at the height of the dog's nose.

Step 3. Before you take the dog out, say "Outside? Do you want to go outside?" Then, ring the bell. Repeat for a few days.

Step 4. When the dog is not watching you, place a little peanut butter or cheese on the bell.

Step 5. When you ask the dog if he wants to go outside, say "Ring the bell." Point at or wiggle the bell if necessary. When the dog gets close to the bell, he will smell the peanut butter. When he licks it off, the bell will ring. Praise him and let the dog outside. Repeat.

Step 6. After the dog learns how to push the bell with his nose, ask the dog "Outside?" and wait by the door until the dog "rings" the bell. Immediately, praise him and let him outside.

This trick teaches dogs to use their behavior to get what they want.

Red rings a bell to indicate he needs to go outside.

PlaySMART and Develop the Whole Dog

Dogs are wonder-full. You wonder how you can survive until they grow up. At work, you wonder what they are doing at home. At home, you wonder how they find the energy for leaping in the air, racing through hallways, and chasing after fleet-footed children or hurtling toys. You wonder how you will ever housetrain this swift, funny, happy, carefree canine.

Working with a dog involves more than housetraining. Learning the house rules is one of the building blocks of your relationship. However, developing rapport, listening, and learning together are the raw materials that form the foundation.

The best way I know to deal with the housetraining process is to work with the whole dog; not just his bathroom habits. Playing games, teaching sit, and practicing tricks help me keep housetraining in perspective. Dogs are my companions, friends, and happy tricksters. And I want to keep them that way.

19 | **Habit Forming Tip:** Plan schooling sessions and choose activities to build a relationship that will last a lifetime.

*When your dog has eyes for
you, anything is possible!*

CHAPTER 8

• • • • • • • • • •

Retraining the Resistant Dog

Red Sun Rising, my golden retriever, is a rescue dog whom I acquired from our local animal shelter five years ago. After I brought Red home with me, I quickly learned the reasons for his stint "behind bars." Red was 10 months old, hyperactive, and his idea of a good time was to run, jump, and use his 65 pounds to body slam me or my husband. Most important, he was not housetrained.

The day I brought Red home, he slipped out of the shelter's collar and raced inside to the living room as soon as I opened the door to the house. Then, while I closed and locked the front door, Red graced my beige living room carpeting with three king-size loafs.

With one action, Red made it clear to me why his previous family left him at the shelter.

We think that because dogs live with us, they are like us, but that is not true. For example, from a dog's perspective, a house contains a significant amount of space. Dogs do not have 45-minute commutes by cars, subways, trains, or buses to their jobs. Their trips are limited to the backyard, around the block, or visits to the park. Distance for them is the space between living room and kitchen. Red intuitively chose a place in my house that was low in traffic and a significant distance from the rest of the house as his toilet area.

If Red was to successfully join my family, I had to look at the world through his golden retriever eyes. It was up to me to teach him new habits. However, I needed to teach him in ways that would maintain his confidence, my self-respect, and our relationship.

20	**Habit Forming Tip:** When you confuse your opinions about a dog's life with the facts of his existence, problems get worse, not better. Remember, *why* dogs act and what you see are not the same.

When we think about retraining dogs, we often get our desires confused with the dogs' needs and wants. For example, because we do not want to tie ourselves to a schedule, we allow a dog to roam unsupervised throughout the house before he is ready for total freedom. Dogs are not aware that there are specific house rules they must follow; they must be taught. Your job is to educate your dog in a non-threatening way to use a specific toilet area so that you both can be happy living at home.

You know what you want; a housetrained dog. Now you need to figure out what part of the initial housetraining was skipped or misunderstood. Once you figure out the missing pieces, then you know where to begin schooling your dog. The secret to effective retraining requires that you practice five basic principles:

- Teach a dog to focus and listen.
- Treat the dog as a first-time learner.
- Use teaching techniques that build a dog's confidence, your self-respect, and the relationship.
- Create schooling sessions to give rewards.
- Practice patience.

21 | **Habit Forming Tip:** Retraining the resistant dog is like putting together the pieces of an intricately designed puzzle. Once you understand the overall picture, then you can identify the smaller pieces that make up each part.

#1: Leaders Teach Dogs to Focus and Listen

Frequently, dogs who soil in the house also do not come, sit, or down. They might jump, bark incessantly, chew, or dig. House-training is just one more instance where the dog does what he wants and ignores you. The easiest way to gain a dog's attention is to be a leader.

Leaders take charge. They initiate, govern, moderate, guide, steer, control, and influence the actions of others. Leaders use their behavior, food, and games to convey to dogs their position as leader. The following actions on your part will demonstrate clearly that you are the leader in your "pack."

Leaders always go first. They walk through doorways and down the stairs before their dogs. Also, leaders have the right of way. If a dog lies in front of a closet door or the opening to the kitchen that you need to enter, the dog must move out of your way. Do not step over or around the dog!

Leaders understand the importance of position and place. They always want a higher physical position than their followers, so dogs should not sleep on beds or sit on furniture.

Leaders control food. They eat first. Leaders never leave out a dog bowl full of food all day. Instead, they require that dogs *earn* their food with a behavior such as a sit-stay *before* they are given permission to eat. In addition, leaders do not hand out treats unless the dog has earned them by performing a specific behavior such as sit, down, come, or roll over.

Leaders start and stop all games. If a dog drops a tennis ball or toy in your lap, leaders say "Not now" and go on with what they are doing. After a minute passes, you can get another tennis ball or favorite toy from a closet or drawer and ask the dog to play with you. Remember, if you play tug-of-war games with your dog, the leader always wins.

Leaders pay attention and reward their dogs for correct behavior. Leaders expect their followers to watch them. When they see a dog focus on them, down, stand, or come on signal, they reward them. Leaders expect dogs to *earn* rewards. If dogs nudge them with their muzzles to demand attention, leaders require dogs to perform a behavior, such as sit or down, before they reward them with a friendly pat.

Dogs who pay attention to their leader learn important listening skills.

#2: Treat the Dog as a First-Time Learner

MAKE NO ASSUMPTIONS ABOUT A DOG'S BEHAVIOR

In order to treat the dog as a first-time learner, you need to uncover the assumptions that affect *your* behavior. For example, you assume that because you installed a doggy door your cairn terrier Misty will use it every time she needs to eliminate. Wrong! Installing a doggy door does not mean that Misty knows how to use it. Successful use requires that you teach Misty and reward her for using the doggy door. Three common assumptions often cause housetraining attempts to fail.

Assumption #1. *Build a better mouse trap.* With this approach, people buy doggy doors, doggy pads, crates, x-pens, and gates and assume that the object will automatically solve all their problems. However, objects do not train dogs, people teach dogs.

Assumption #2. *Once is enough.* Seeing a dog perform a behavior once, twice, or three times does not mean that the dog *knows* what he is supposed to do. Only with repetition and consistent rewards will dogs learn new toilet manners.

Assumption #3. *Hold on, I'm coming.* When we assume that a dog can "hold it" for nine hours or more every day, we forget that Mother Nature has her own rhythms that must be followed. Dogs must eliminate at certain intervals, which is why you need to maintain a feeding, watering, and exercise routine that maximizes a dog's natural inclination to eliminate at a certain time and in the right location.

Treating a dog as a first-time learner requires that you discard any assumptions that the dog understands you, your signals, or rules. Instead, it's time to start over at the beginning. Pick new words, create a schedule, and practice teaching techniques that link the right behavior—puddles and piles in the doggy toilet area—with rewards. The issue in retraining is understanding: Does the dog understand what you want? Remember, dogs can only do what they know; and if they don't know it, they can't do it.

22 | **Habit Forming Tip:** Don't spend time fixing problems; invest time in training.

#3: Use Teaching Methods That Build a Dog's Confidence, Your Self-Respect, and the Relationship

For me, the only way to housetrain a dog is to use positive teaching techniques that build a dog's confidence and maintain your self-respect and the relationship. In other words, you can have rules and still be nice. The key is to understand where the dog is on the learning cycle and not be swept away by anger or frustration. Nice handlers are specialists in praise, petting, affection, and effective directions.

Persistence pays off! Living in Arizona can be a real challenge in housetraining a puppy. With temperatures over 110 degrees, Sierra did not want to go outside. Instead, she used a favorite place on the living room rug. Sierra's handlers learned to stop Sierra in mid squat with one word, "Outside!" and immediately take her out. Once she was in the backyard, lots of praise followed the completion of her puddle or pile. Now Sierra is 18 months old; however, she was completely housetrained at four months.

Dogs learn best when they feel physically safe and emotionally secure. Emotional rollercoaster rides where the handler is happy and bouncy one moment, then angry or mean the next confuse dogs and create uncertainty. Nice handlers don't kick the dog after a bad day. Instead, they realize that consistent positive acts on their part generate good results, so they emphasize the positive. They develop intelligent, friendly techniques to increase a dog's trust. Then, they can work with the dog's awareness and ability to eliminate in the right location.

 If a dog eliminates in an inappropriate place, effective handlers do not blame the dog. Instead, they search until they discover what they, as handlers, ignored, forgot, or assumed. By looking within, they find the best way out.

#4: Design Schooling Sessions to Give Rewards

EMPLOY BEHAVIOR-BASED SOLUTIONS

Creating situations where no one loses is the secret to effective housetraining. It can be summed up in two words, "Be prepared." All it requires is a little thinking on your part to size up the situation and structure it so that your dog will succeed on his first try. For example, design a feeding, watering, and exercise schedule that maximizes a dog's natural inclination to eliminate at the correct time and in the right location.

Luckily, dogs like rewards. It is easy to create lessons so that your dog will earn a reward when he performs a specific behavior. For example, if you want your dog to bark in order to tell you that he needs to go out, teach him how to use his barking to get your attention.

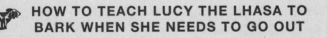 **HOW TO TEACH LUCY THE LHASA TO BARK WHEN SHE NEEDS TO GO OUT**

Face the dog.

Step 1. Teach the dog to bark by acting excited: make noises, use a high-pitched tone of voice, wiggle your fingers, wave your arms, or squeak a toy. As soon as the dog barks, say "Good bark. Outside?!"

Step 2. Take the dog outside.

Step 3. Say "Go potty!" As she eliminates, repeat the words "Go potty" in a friendly, happy voice so that she recognizes that she is being praised.

In a short time the dog will associate barking with you opening the door, so she can go outside to eliminate.

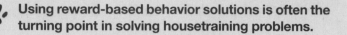

Using reward-based behavior solutions is often the turning point in solving housetraining problems.

#5: Practice Patience

Do Not Give Up Too Soon

Many people follow a policy of too little, too late. Teaching dogs where and when to eliminate is not as complicated as you think. If you are willing to take the time, you will get good results.

Practicing patience is like owning a sled in the summertime. If you wait long enough, the snow will come. So too, with dogs. In the same way that you cannot force snow to appear in July, you cannot force your dog to be housetrained before his time. However, you can seed the clouds, and in time, rain turns to sleet, which turns to snow. It's important to remember on day four of your housetraining program that in eight more days your dog will be completely housetrained.

Hurrying does not make things happen faster. In fact, when you hurry, schooling often takes longer. The lament of impatient people is "I don't have time for this! Oh no! He pooped as soon as we came back inside the house!"

I remember when I first started Red Sun Rising's housetraining program. Red joined our family two weeks before I was leaving on a business trip. It was not the most convenient time for me to add an untrained adolescent. In addition to my regular work day, I had many extra tasks in order to prepare for the trip. I will never forget standing for one to two hours every time I took Red outside to potty. In the mornings, afternoons, and evenings, I stood in an open, grassy area with Red on a 15-foot yellow line waiting for him to eliminate so I could associate the word "tinkletime" as he peed, then praise and reward him. I could not hurry Red. He was a nervous, hyper, rescue dog. Any attempts for me to hurry or force him would increase his anxiety level, not decrease it. In order to eliminate, Red needed to feel calm, relaxed, and unpressured.

Retraining is inconvenient. However, the actions you take today will affect what happens tomorrow, next week, and next month. If I had become impatient or attempted to hurry Red, the pressure would have lengthened, not shortened, our training time, so I waited quietly and watched. My patience was rewarded. Red was a completely housetrained dog in just 10 days.

 SEVEN REASONS WHY HOUSETRAINING FAILS

1. No mistakes permitted; instant and constant perfection demanded.
2. Improper corrections and punishment.
3. Poor planning; not enough potty breaks at the right time.
4. Lack of supervision inside and outside.
5. Too much freedom too soon.
6. Haphazard training methods; each family member uses different teaching techniques.
7. No praise when dog eliminates in the right place.

When Things Don't Go as Planned . . .

Marie had a perfect 5-year-old standard poodle named Paris. However, when Marie moved to a different house, Paris started marking and wetting in different parts of the house. Marie knew that the house had been repainted and the carpets cleaned before she moved in. What Marie did not realize was that the previous family had two dogs and three cats who used the entire house as their toilet area. Paris was just following his natural instincts to re-mark an area where another animal's scent remained.

Carpet cleaning could not remove the smell and odor that was firmly established in the carpet's padding. Marie finally solved her dilemma by removing the carpeting, cleaning and sealing the cement, and installing new carpeting.

Sometimes even the best dog can have problems. If your perfectly trained dog suddenly starts experiencing housesoiling problems, ask yourself what has changed. For example, has your workday changed from days to evenings? Have you added any new animals to your house such as a cat, rabbit, guinea pig, or another dog? Did you get married, add a roommate, or have a baby? Did you move to a home where the previous occupant had animals? Is there a loose dog or stray cat in your neighborhood? Is your dog sick with a urinary tract infection? Answers can be as obvious as the nose on a saluki's face. All you have to do is stop, pay attention, and figure out what has changed.

To learn how to solve specific housetraining problems, turn to the next chapter.

CHAPTER 9

• • • • • • • • • • •

Fourteen Common
Housesoiling Problems
and Their Solutions

Accidents happen. Dogs with diarrhea cannot hold their bowels until you arrive home from work. Puppy bladders empty according to their schedule, not yours. However, there is a difference between an accident and an established behavior pattern. Accidents are random, one-time events. A behavior pattern consistently repeats the same action.

Keep in mind that the problem may have started before the dog ever came to your house. For example, the role of the pet store or breeder is critical. If they did not pick up soiled papers and replace them with clean ones, puppies can learn to play and sleep in a dirty environment. Once puppies accept soiled papers as normal, they do not have any impetus to keep their areas clean. Dogs who lived in filthy kennels and puppies who grew up in dirty surroundings can take longer to learn house manners.

If the dog has been part of your family for a while without any problems, review the dog's diet, health, and environment for any factors that could cause the dog to change his elimination habits. For example, have you changed dog food? Is the dog ill?

23 | **Habit Forming Tip:** If you get frustrated, find a dog trainer or behaviorist to help you with your dog. They're experts at solving training issues quickly and efficiently.

On medication? Did you change houses or apartments? Add another animal? Lose a family member? Did your work schedule alter? Change and stress can affect any dog's elimination habits. However, every problem has a solution. The key is to figure out the reasons behind the dog's actions, and what you need to teach in order for the dog to change his behavior. Returning to the basics usually solves most problems. For example, create a schedule, teach a signal, and reward the dog for eliminating. Remember, threats don't work. You must find ways to praise and reward the dog for puddles and piles in the right place.

This chapter covers 14 major housesoiling problems and their solutions. The first section covers 10 housetraining issues. The second section covers four papertraining situations.

Housetraining

BATHROOM BREAKDOWNS

Previously housetrained dogs who suddenly start having accidents require your immediate attention. Multiple accidents can signal health problems, unresolved behavior issues, or lifestyle changes. If an accident happens only once, it may simply be a timing issue—the dog could not hold it any longer and had to relieve herself. Until we teach dogs to use the family toilet, we must accept our responsibility to provide dogs with an appropriate schedule.

Key Point. Unexpected accidents always have a cause. Your job is to figure out the facts or circumstances that have resulted in a bathroom breakdown. Then you can make the necessary changes so the dog can be accident-free again.

Step 1. Evaluate the dog's health. Visit your veterinarian. Urinary tract infections can turn perfectly housetrained dogs into gushing fountains. Dogs can also lose control due to health problems such as diarrhea, tumors, cysts, hormonal problems, too much vitamin C, or side effects from medication, as well as old-age health issues such as poor muscle control.

Step 2. Examine the dog's behavior. If the veterinarian rules out any health problems, then you need to search for any situational changes that could affect your dog's behavior. For example, does the dog no longer have access to a doggy door? Have you moved and the dog now lives in an apartment in the city instead of in a house in the suburbs? Is the dog afraid to go outside because a neighbor's dogs bark and growl at the chain-link fence that separates your yards? Once you determine the reason behind the dog's behavior, you can take steps to improve the situation.

Step 3. Check for any lifestyle changes. Ask yourself if you have experienced any lifestyle changes that could influence your dog's behavior. For example, did your work schedule alter so that you work longer hours and cannot let your dog out in a timely manner? (Pages 20–21 discuss how to use assistants such as dog walkers when you are too busy.) Have you added a new animal into the house? (Pages 126–128 cover territorial marking.) Do you have house guests? Did a son or daughter leave for college?

DIRTIES DEN

Puppies learn at an early age not to soil where they live. During the first three weeks their mothers not only stimulate a newborn puppy's ability to eliminate, they also clean up after them immediately. Soon puppies learn to leave the nest to eliminate.

Puppies who grow up in a clean environment do not want to dirty their den.

Most dogs soil their crates for two reasons. First, the puppy lives in a crate that is so big, she can create separate living and toilet areas. Second, the crate is the right size, but the puppy or dog is left inside it too long and has no choice but to dirty her den.

Key Point. Floor space and the amount of time spent inside a crate are important considerations when crate training puppies or dogs.

Step 1. Prevent the problem. If the crate is too big, buy a new crate or create a partition so that the dog has less floor space. Crates should be large enough so that the dog can stand up, turn around, and lie down.

Step 2. Check your schedule. How much time does the dog spend inside the crate? Puppies and dogs need regular potty and play breaks. Remember, crates are *temporary* training

---

 HOW TO MAKE A TEMPORARY WALL FOR YOUR VINYL CRATE*

Step 1. Find a box that is slightly smaller than your crate.

Step 2. Fasten a ¼-inch piece of plywood to one side of the box to create a strong divider that a dog cannot push through.

Step 3. Find a heavy weight to place inside the box, so that the box cannot be easily moved. For example, use heavy phone books, bricks, or cement blocks.

Step 4. Place the box in the far end of the crate.

*If you have a wire crate, buy wire mesh and use it as a divider.

measures. They are not a substitute for teaching a dog manners. A crate's effectiveness depends on how you use it.

Step 3. Eliminate using a crate. Start the house-training process over. This time use a small room or x-pen with papers covering the floor. Follow a set feeding, watering, and exercise program.

EATS FECES/COPROPHAGY

When the dog who licks your face is the same dog who eats feces, it's time to find a way to stop this habit. Not only is feces-eating unappealing, it can also indicate digestive problems. This habit also carries potential health risks if parasite-infested dog, cat, or bird feces is eaten.

Key Point. Eating feces can be stopped in four ways: prevent the problem, alter the dog's diet, eliminate boredom, or teach the dog to "leave it."

Step 1. Prevent the problem. How clean is your yard? If you clean up each time after your dog defecates, there will be no piles for your dog to eat.

Step 2. Alter the dog's diet. If a dog's digestive system functions effectively, nutrients in food are broken down, absorbed, and used. However, some dogs have poor digestive systems. Their bodies do not process food efficiently, which means their feces contain undigested nutrients. These dogs often eat their stools to gain the nutrients they are missing. Hungry dogs will eat feces. With a veterinarian's assistance you can analyze your dog's digestive system, add the appropriate digestive enzymes, change to a more complete dog food, or give vitamin and mineral supplements to provide the nutrition that your dog requires.

Step 3. Eliminate boredom. Dogs who are left alone too long, lack exercise, and live in a yard full of feces can also eat piles. Bitter Apple®, vinegar, cayenne pepper, or strong mouthwash can be sprayed over the piles. However, this after-the-fact approach is not usually effective. It is much easier to keep the

HOW TO TEACH MELODY THE SHELTIE TO "LEAVE IT!"

In order to teach "Leave it" you must first teach "Take it."

Step 1. Place a treat in your open palm. Drop your hand to dog nose level. Say "Melody, take it." Repeat.

Step 2. Place a treat in your open palm. As Melody comes up, fold your fingers over the treat. Say "Leave it." In the beginning Melody will not understand what you mean. After all, she can smell the treat. After a few seconds most dogs will quit sniffing your hand. However, If Melody continues to nudge, worry, or "glue" herself to your hand for the treat, shake your hand quickly and say "Leave it" again in a lower, stronger voice. If Melody still goes after your hand, ignore her. Eventually, her nose will back off. As soon as it does, say "Take it!" and open your hand so Melody can eat the treat.

Step 3. Repeat "Take it" and "Leave it" until Melody willingly keeps her distance from your closed hand.

Step 4. Repeat the exercise but this time do not cover the treat with your fingers during the "Leave it" exercise. Once Melody succeeds consistently with this exercise, you are ready for the next step.

Step 5. Place an object on the ground that Melody likes but is not crazy about. For example, use a few pieces of her dry kibble, but not her favorite ball. Stand near the object.

Step 6. As Melody approaches, tell her "Leave it." If she looks at it and walks away, praise and reward her. If Melody looks and goes to eat it, quickly hide it with your foot, or bend down and cover it with your hand. Say "Leave it!" Repeat the exercise.

Once the dog understands "Leave it" you can stop her from eating a pile in your presence.

dog's yard clean. In addition, give the dog more toys to play with or bones to chew, and take the dog on walks.

Step 4. Teach the dog to "Leave it!" When you take your dog on walks, or when the dog runs free, if he knows the signal "Leave it!" he will not sniff, linger, or eat a pile.

ELIMINATES INSIDE HOUSE IMMEDIATELY AFTER A WALK OUTSIDE

In order to solve this situation, you must determine if your dog is a Shy Sally, a Sneaky Pete, or an Ask Alice. "Shy Sally"s are afraid to go outside because loud noises, traffic, crowded sidewalks, busy parks, loose cats, or other dogs inhibit them. Without confidence, they cannot easily eliminate. They wait until they are in the security of their own home to pee or poop.

"Sneaky Pete"s are dogs who have been harshly reprimanded for leaving a puddle or pile in the wrong spot. They have learned that if they eliminate in front of you, they will be punished. Sneaky Petes do not associate punishment with the act of elimination, but with you. Now, they wait until you cannot see them, and then go potty.

"Ask Alice"s are dogs who never learned the difference between a walk and a trip to the bathroom. Ask Alices are completely unaware of what you want them to do. Their initial housetraining lessons were not clear and they do not understand what you want.

Key Point. You cannot work with an event that does not happen in your presence. Dogs who won't go outside because they are afraid of the environment, dogs who make mistakes out of sight because they are scared of your reaction, and dogs who have no idea of what behavior is desired, all have one thing in common—your teaching did not give them the knowledge or confidence to eliminate outside in your presence.

Step 1. Shy Sallys. Shy Sallys need confidence-building lessons and positive exposure to the out-of-doors. One of the best ways I know to build confidence in a shy dog is to find an activity that allows them to feel a sense of accomplishment. I like to teach shy or timid dogs to use their bodies in new ways; for example, to jump through a hoop or my arms, run over a course of jumps, sprint through a tunnel, or walk on an upraised board on signal. It's easy to buy a hula hoop, make a hurdle out of a broom handle on blocks, place a 10-inch-wide board on books, or create a tunnel out of cardboard boxes or pillowcases draped over the sides of small tables or chairs. These activities can be done on a small scale inside the house or in the backyard. (I have one client who places dog jumps between doorways in her apartment.) Once your Shy Sally is comfortable in one location, the next step is to perform the activities in different places such as the front yard, a neighbor's yard, and the park. The final step is to add admiring guests who chat, talk, and eventually bring their dogs to watch Sally demonstrate her talents.

As Shy Sallys learn to focus their attention and perform, outside events influence them less. Greater confidence enables them to concentrate on finding the right spot to eliminate. However, they still need plenty of cover—bushes, trees, boulders, or flowers. In addition, you can use a long or retractable leash to increase their privacy. After they consistently eliminate outside without any problems, you can start shortening the leash. If possible, take Shy Sallys out during times when there is less noise and confusion; even Central Park in New York City is fairly quiet early in the morning.

Step 2. Sneaky Petes. It's easy to determine if your dog is afraid to eliminate in your presence. First, ask yourself, did you yell, hit Pete, or rub his nose in a pile when you caught him eliminating in the wrong location? How many times did you punish Pete? How many times have you seen Pete eliminate in your presence recently? Dogs who are wary of people's reactions avoid them.

In order to solve this situation, you need to rebuild your relationship. Go back to the beginning. Teach Pete that your presence means rewards, not reprimands. For example, teach Pete a trick such as roll over, or work on simple exercises such as sit or down. Use these sessions to teach Pete that he can earn *performance* rewards. Once Pete associates your presence with praise, rewards, fun and games, you can start the housetraining process again.

Step 3. Ask Alices. Ask Alices need to learn the difference between a walk and a potty break. Confused dogs need very structured lessons that leave no room for misinterpretation. By using behavior-based reward training, you can teach Alice that puddles and piles belong in a specific location. To clear up any uncertainties always follow the same routine; use the same stairs, the same door, and go to the same place. Once your dog eliminates 25 times in one area at your request, change to a different location.

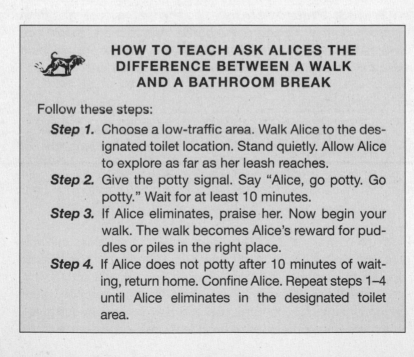

HOW TO TEACH ASK ALICES THE DIFFERENCE BETWEEN A WALK AND A BATHROOM BREAK

Follow these steps:

Step 1. Choose a low-traffic area. Walk Alice to the designated toilet location. Stand quietly. Allow Alice to explore as far as her leash reaches.

Step 2. Give the potty signal. Say "Alice, go potty. Go potty." Wait for at least 10 minutes.

Step 3. If Alice eliminates, praise her. Now begin your walk. The walk becomes Alice's reward for puddles or piles in the right place.

Step 4. If Alice does not potty after 10 minutes of waiting, return home. Confine Alice. Repeat steps 1–4 until Alice eliminates in the designated toilet area.

FAVORITE SPOTS

Some dogs do not only potty outside, they also use specific toilet areas inside the house. Favorite spots are locations that dogs return to for puddles and piles. They are normally located in hidden areas, far away from where dogs play, sleep, or eat.

Key Point. Unsupervised dogs who received inadequate housetraining instructions, as well as dogs who lack regularly scheduled bathroom and exercise breaks, often develop favorite indoor toilet areas.

Step 1. Check your schedule. Dogs cannot always "hold it" to fit your schedule. If you work long hours, find someone who can give your dog a bathroom break.

Step 2. Add new training tools. Add a doggy door and teach your dog how to use it. Buy a crate or an x-pen. (To learn about doggy doors, crates, and x-pens, see pages 36–43.)

Step 3. Stake a claim. Change that favorite spot from an isolated area to a part of the house. Ask your dog to join you at the "favorite spot" for daily scratching, playing, or teaching sessions. After your session, place another water dish there.

> 🐾 Remember, dogs do not soil in areas where they eat, drink, play, or claim as their personal property.

LEG LIFTING/SCENT MARKING/ TERRITORIAL MARKING

Intact male dogs often lift their legs to mark territory. Other dogs start scent marking with the arrival of a new animal, baby, or houseguest. You might have accidentally encouraged your dog in leg lifting if you permitted and praised your dog to mark every tree, fire hydrant, bush, sign, or "post" he encounters.

Key Point. In order to solve this situation you need to figure out the dog's attitude. Why is the dog marking? Then, you can determine your approach.

Problem #1—Marking Territory When You Are Not Home. For chronic leg lifters one of the best steps is to neuter the dog. Frequently, neutering solves the problem, especially when it is combined with the following steps.

Step 1. Evaluate the outside environment. Determine if the dog is marking because of activities outside your house from stray dogs or cats, children playing, or road, utility, or home construction. To diminish the effect of external stressful activities, close the blinds and turn on the radio. If possible keep the dog out of the rooms closest to the commotion.

Step 2. Evaluate the inside environment. Determine if the dog marks because of activity inside the house. If the dog fights with his siblings or chases cats and marks to show territory, you must first deal with his attitude before you can alter the dog's behavior. Often an attitude readjustment solves the leg lifting behavior. Seek professional assistance to help you solve territorial issues.

Step 3. Remove as many urination posts as possible. Attach aluminum foil or Saran wrap to prevent the dog from marking a table leg, chair cushion, plant stands, or wastepaper baskets. Many dogs do not like nonabsorbent surfaces that splash them. Once you have dog-proofed the room, then you can confine the dog when you are not home or are unable to watch him. Another alternative is to confine the dog in a crate or exercise-pen. However, whenever you limit a dog's freedom, you must design a feeding, watering, exercise, and playing schedule and follow it consistently.

 Note. You should only use a crate if you can provide *frequent* exercise and play times.

Problem #2—Marking Territory When You Are Home. If the dog marks while you are home, do not allow him to wander unsupervised throughout the house.

Step 1. Use a waist leash. A waist leash keeps the dog close to you. This usually prevents a dog from marking. However, if you see the dog lift his leg, redirect him. Say "Outside!" Immediately take the dog outside and tell him to "Go potty." If the dog wets, reward him.

Step 2. Practice your leadership skills. One of my clients had a protection-trained Rottweiler whom she was forced to keep in her laundry room because he marked throughout her house. Since the dog was obedience trained, I suggested that she have the dog perform an obedience routine that required the dog to sit at every spot where he had previously marked. The next morning she started the dog's day with his new routine. The dog's leg lifting stopped the same day. I have asked other dogs to perform tricks, play games, or experience relaxing, touching and rubbing bodywork sessions at previously marked areas. These activities help dogs to recognize an area as theirs. When an area is "claimed" the dog does not experience the same need to mark it. The more times a day you practice the session, the quicker the dog claims a location. To confirm the dog's avoidance of an area, place a food dish or a bowl of water at the area when you finish the session, since dogs do not eliminate where they eat or drink.

Sandra uses a waist-leash with Cody to limit his freedom.

OLDER DOGS/FAILING MEMORY

As dogs age their bodies change accordingly. Eyes cloud with cataracts and their vision diminishes. Ears once sensitive to the slightest sound no longer hear the buzz of the can opener slicing through the lid of their favorite dog food. Strong legs no longer jump or leap, but push with effort as they change from lying down to standing up. Weakening muscle elasticity often affects older dogs' ability to control their bladder or bowels. When dogs are unable to physically hold it, they soil in the house.

Key Point. Older dogs need more of our attention, not less. We must fit our schedule and adapt our living conditions to meet their special needs.

24 | **Habit Forming Tip:** Be Proactive! Keep your dog in shape. Use diet and exercise to help maintain muscle tone.

Step 1. Enlist your veterinarian's help to resolve any health problems. Find out if there is a medical reason for the dog's soiling in the house. Talk to your veterinarian. She can help you understand if the problem is due to a hormone imbalance, weakened muscles, urinary tract infection, or other health problems such as diabetes. She can also suggest appropriate medications.

Step 2. Change the dog's physical environment. Ask yourself, can your older dog get through the doggy door or walk down the steps to the backyard? You can always buy a bigger doggy door or build a ramp.

If the dog needs more frequent potty breaks, install a doggy door and teach her to use it. (See page 42.) If you cannot install a doggy door, paper- or litter-box-train the dog. Find someone to help you. Hire a pet walker. Ask family or friends to give your dog a potty break.

Older dogs can dribble or leak from lack of muscle control. However, you can use doggy diapers or place doggy pads where the dog usually lies down so that when the dog leaks, the urine does not stain the carpet, tile, or wood floor.

Step 3. Treat the forgetful dog like a puppy. Does your dog walk outside, pause, sniff, look around, walk back inside and eliminate? Older dogs can forget basic behaviors. Dogs with failing memories require that you take them out and tell them that it's time to do their business. Treat your dog like a puppy. Give her the potty signal, watch her, and praise her. Increase the frequency of her bathroom breaks, or use doggy diapers.

> 🐾 **You may not want to give the forgetful dog free run inside the house when you are not home. Instead, confine her to a room that has papers or a litter box in it when you are away.**

PUDDLES AND PILES DURING THE NIGHT

There is a definite cycle to the elimination process. It involves both the aging process as well as a dog's natural biorhythms. For example, as puppies mature, their ability to "hold it" usually increases. We just have to wait until a puppy's body develops. Dogs, like people, must evacuate their systems at specific intervals during the day. Fluids and fecal matter cannot be held back once they reach a certain point.

Key Point. Adult dogs who consistently need to go out in the middle of the night need to have their food, water, and exercise schedule evaluated. Puppies require middle-of-the-night potty breaks until their bodies mature.

Step 1. Observe your dog. Watch your dog. Does he eliminate when you let him out in the backyard? Or does he just run around and sniff? It's easy to turn on the floodlights, watch out a window, or put on a jacket to walk outside to make sure the dog potties before he comes inside for the night.

Step 2. Change your dog's schedule. When you feed your dog can make a critical difference to his toilet habits. Try feeding your dog at 9 or 10 P.M. instead of 6 P.M. If that stops his nighttime puddles and piles, keep the dog on this schedule for at least one month. If you want to return your dog to an earlier eating schedule, move up his dinnertime meal by 15-minute increments.

Step 3. Add training tools. Add a doggy door and teach the dog how to use it. (To learn about doggy doors, turn to page 42.)

Refuses to Potty in the Rain, Snow, or on a Wet Lawn

I live in the high Sonoran desert. Today, for the first time in Red's five-year-old life it snowed. Big, white, fluffy flakes. At first Red stayed on our back deck, unwilling to go outside for his bathroom break. Then I said, "Red, let's play ball!" and threw a tennis ball. Red leaped through the air chasing the ball. Running after tennis balls is one of Red's favorite activities. Red paid no attention to the snowflakes that landed on his nose, face, and back. After all, this was game time. As soon as Red could ignore the snow, I knew he would have no problems when I told him, "Red. Go tinkle. Tinkletime." Sure enough, I signaled Red to do his business and, standing in slush by the palo verde tree, Red lifted his leg and peed.

Key Point. Dogs can learn to eliminate in any type of weather. All it takes is your imagination, the right games or rewards, rain or snow outfits for you and your dog, and patience.

Step 1. Prevent the problem. If you know your dog does not like to get his paws wet, play games or teach new tricks on wet grass or muddy ground. For example, does your dog like to play ball? Chase after a toy? Can he shake hands, walk through your legs in a figure eight, balance a treat on his nose, or catch a Frisbee? Dogs who are busy concentrating on performing a trick or playing a game do not let wet, snowy, or muddy paws prevent them from having fun and earning rewards. Once dogs learn that good things happen in bad weather, they lose their inhibitions about getting wet or cold, and muddy or slick footing.

25 | **Habit Forming Tip:** Don't wait for a rainstorm to work on the dog's behavior. Water your lawn and bring out your dog for a play session in the wet grass. Or, take your dog on a walk after the grass in the park is watered. When it finally rains use every rainstorm as an excuse to pee, poop, and play. Dogs quickly learn that wet, sticky, or snowy paws often are the forerunners to fun.

Step 2. Be practical. Buy doggy boots and a raincoat or sweater for your dog. Find a large umbrella that covers both of you. Use them. If your dog doesn't feel wet or cold, he won't be bothered by the weather. Then you can wait in comfort.

Step 3. Change your attitude. Dogs are masters at picking up what we really think. If you are muttering to yourself, "I hate this. It's raining. Now, I'll get wet. I hate walking in the rain," your dog won't like rain either. You don't have to be a Gene Kelly and sing in the rain, but you can change your tune. Figure out what you can do that will turn a bad weather day into a good experience for you. For example, bring a covered mug of hot cocoa, coffee, or lemonade with you. Or, ask one of your kids to come with you and use it as a time to catch up on the latest news.

Springing a Leak/Submissive Urination

Dogs roll over and pee or stand up and dribble urine as an *automatic* response to a dominant person or dog. Submissive urination can happen when you or your friends come into your house, while you are scolding the dog, in response to arguments between you and another person, or in the presence of a new dog.

Key Point. Corrections of any type do not work with submissive urination. Dogs submissively urinate to appease the more dominant individual. These dogs are sensitive souls who cannot handle corrections, especially harsh ones. Any corrections, discipline, or anger reassert your dominant position and cause the dog to feel *more* submissive. This magnifies the problem, since it's the dog's lack of confidence that initially caused the situation. To solve this problem you must find ways to decrease the dog's anxiety and increase his confidence.

Step 1. Change the way you greet your dog. If your dog springs a leak when you come home, recognize the dog with a friendly greeting, "Hi, Friar," but do not pat him on his head or make eye contact with him. Patting a dog on the head stresses your dominant position. Your body bends over and your hand comes from space far above the dog's head and presses down on him as you tower over him.

Avoid eye contact because dogs use eye contact to determine rank; averted eyes indicate that the other dog has a higher rank. Instead, keep moving. Hang up your coat, walk into the bedroom and change clothes, or go to the kitchen for a snack. You have increased the probability that your dog will not submissively urinate because your constant movement prevents him from making eye contact with you, staying in one place, and peeing.

Another possibility is to greet the dog when you come home and then toss him a Kong, ball, treat, toy, or rawhide. You have two goals with tossing a surprise. The first goal is to redirect

Friar's attention away from you to something very interesting. The second goal is to eliminate any anxiety on Friar's part and replace it with something joyful.

Step 2. Change where you greet your dog. Greet Friar in the yard instead of inside the house. Often by changing where a dog greets you, you can eliminate his submissive urination. For example, if you have a doggy door that opens into a fenced yard, walk into the yard, call Friar's name, and have him greet you outside. Be friendly but don't go wild with your greetings.

Step 3. Build your dog's confidence. Use positive teaching methods. Find ways to increase the dog's confidence. For example, play games such as Find-the-toy or Catch a ball, that the dog wins. Teach your dog tricks such as Jump through my arms or Go through a tunnel. Whenever possible, bend your knees or sit on the floor; try to meet the dog at his level when you work with him.

Step 4. Remove the stress. If a dog submissively urinates when you are having a disagreement with another person, move to a different room. Before you leave, turn on the radio or the television to cover the intensity of angry voices.

Papertraining

CANNOT FIND THE PAPERS

There are two important aspects to papertraining. Your first task is to teach the dog to use papers when he needs to relieve himself. The second task requires that you teach the dog to only use papers in a specific area. Dogs who eliminate in unacceptable locations have not learned to tie the act of eliminating to a specific target area.

Key Point. Dogs who eliminate on papers other than the designated ones must be taught to find the right papers.

Step 1. Teach the dog to "Find the papers!"

Dogs can easily be taught how to find the papers from any area in the house if you turn it into a game.

First. Start close to the papers. Ask the dog to sit-stay about two feet from the papers. While the dog watches, throw a treat on the papers. Release the dog. Say "Find the papers!" Repeat.

 Note. If your dog cannot sit-stay, hold your dog with one hand and toss the treat with your other hand.

Second. Without the dog observing you, place a treat on the papers. Then tell the dog "Find the papers!" Repeat.

Third. Increase the dog's distance from the papers until no matter where the dog is he can "Find the papers!" when asked.

Fourth. Once the dog understands where the papers are located, add the signal "Go potty!" after the dog arrives at the papers. Praise and reward.

NEAR MISSES

Dogs who aim for the proper papers and miss, just need to improve their aim. Near misses are one of the easier situations to correct. All it takes is a little rearranging of the toilet area.

Key Point. The dog knows about toilet areas; however, you need to define its location better.

Step 1. Practice good clean-up.

Do not forget to clean up any near misses with an odor neutralizer. Avoid using any cleaners with an ammonia base, since ammonia has a similar smell to urine.

Step 2. Create a larger toilet area. Dogs need space to turn around, sniff, or circle. Check to see that your dog has enough room. It's easy to lay down more papers.

Step 3. Leave a scent marker. Dogs follow their noses and return to the same areas to eliminate. After you put down clean papers, place a lightly soiled paper between the clean papers to lure the dog back.

TEARS UP PAPERS

Dogs who tear up papers usually need more excitement, exercise, and stimulation in their lives. Dogs cannot sleep all day while you are away; they must do something. Ask yourself how you can change the dog's environment so that her attention focuses on other items and activities while you are gone.

Key Point. Increasing the opportunities for play, exercise, and stimulating activities when you are not home eliminates any need to tear up papers.

Step 1. Increase the dog's exercise. Take the dog out on a walk before you leave in the morning. Hire a petwalker or ask a neighbor, friend, or family member to walk and play with your dog during the day.

Step 2. Buy toys that occupy the dog's mind. Toys like Buster Cubes or Kongs harness a dog's attention, creativity, and chewing in positive ways.

Step 3. Cycle your current toys. Dogs like variety. To avoid making constant runs to the toy department, recycle old toys into new toys. Every day remove an "old" toy and replace it with a previously hidden "new" toy. If possible, I like to remove toys for at least one, preferably two weeks, before the dog sees them again.

Step 4. Prevent the problem. Arrange the papers into a neat pile. Then, tape their edges to the floor.

Uses Papers After a Walk

Dogs who are papertrained learn that it is acceptable to eliminate inside the house. It is only natural that they use papers after a walk if they have not been taught to go potty outside.

Key Point. Papertrained dogs must be taught to use the out-of-doors as an additional toilet area.

Step 1. Teach the dog to eliminate outside. You will need to start the housetraining process all over again. However, this time your emphasis will be on teaching your dog to eliminate outside. Chapter 3 covers this method in detail.

CHAPTER 10

• • • • • • • • • •

Your Dog Can Do It!

I never know when the realization will appear during a lesson. However, it inevitably comes and usually sounds like this, "It's not the dog that needs training, it's me. Wow! When I understand, so does he. It's so easy!" As soon as I hear those words, I know the housetraining issue that caused the person to seek my advice will soon disappear.

If you want to learn how easy it is to teach a new behavior or change a habit, move your watch to the opposite wrist for the next 14 days. At first you will automatically look at your left wrist because that is where the watch was located. A few people never look at their left wrist again. Most people need three or four days before they consistently look for the watch on their right wrist. Some people need nine or ten days. What if every time you looked at the watch on your right hand, you received a 100-dollar bill? Would you learn faster? You bet.

Teaching dogs your house rules requires that you change some of their basic behaviors. In the same way that you are accustomed to looking at your left wrist for your watch, dogs are in the habit of eliminating when they have the urge. Effective housetraining requires that dogs delay their basic, immediate needs and wait while they walk through the condo lobby to reach the out-of-doors, exit through a doggy door to the back-yard, or wait for you to open their crate and take them outside. Asking dogs to notify you, eliminate on signal, or eliminate without any supervision is a complicated series of behaviors. That's why the following five ideas are so valuable. They help you housetrain your dogs with less stress and more success in just 14 days.

Idea #1: Concentrate Your Training Efforts

IT ELIMINATES FRUSTRATION AND THE DOG CAN BE INDEPENDENT SOONER

Frank's son, Randy, is learning to drive their F150 Ford pickup truck. Every day I see Frank and Randy driving around the neighborhood. I watch as Randy successfully negotiates parallel parking, slow stops, and moving traffic. Today Randy takes the road test for his driver's license; final proof that he knows the rules of the road and has the skill to drive alone. Randy recognizes that as he handles greater responsibilities safely, Frank will give him more opportunities to drive.

Successful housetraining is like learning to drive a car. In the same way that parents do not permit novice drivers to operate a car without their supervision, dog handlers cannot expect their dogs to target a doggy toilet area without their active participation. In 14 days you can have a housetrained dog, if you concentrate your efforts. Just think. In exchange for 14 days of your time, you can come home to a clean house and a happy dog forever.

26 | **Habit Forming Tip:** Don't throw away your time. Instead, take advantage of the time you have available: take a few days off work, ask friends or family to help you, or hire a pet walker. In the same way you would not attempt to squeeze your foot into a shoe that is two sizes too small, do not attempt to cram your dog's housetraining experience into one or two days.

Idea #2: Teach It Right the First Time, and Dogs Will Do It Right the Rest of Their Lives

Inside the word "dog" are the letters "d" and "o" or "do." "Do" is a small word, yet it carries an impact like the aftershock of a 7.5 earthquake. I like the word "do" because it implies cause and effect in only two letters.

The word "do" recognizes that housetraining is a process, and that you affect what happens next. Dogs must eliminate. The point is to control when and where it occurs. The secret to housetraining is to understand that housetraining is not your dog's responsibility, but yours. Your challenge is to figure out the best housetraining methods for you and your dog. Every situation is different, so find what works for you. Observe the dog's behavior. Examine your schedule. Improvise. Be creative. Enlist help. Once you figure out what must be done, act on it. Your dog can do it. Are you ready to teach your dog?

27 | **Habit Forming Tip:** There is just one shortcut to housetraining—do it right the first time.

Idea #3: Make Your Dog a Winner

Last Friday after an obedience and agility lesson, Diane said to me, "Sheba likes working with you. You make her feel good. You're happy. You notice her and reward her efforts immediately, which keeps her trying harder."

Who likes to lose? Not me. Not your dog. Winning, and being recognized for their efforts immediately makes dogs want to perform. Rewards are like applause to an actor. They teach the dog he's doing something right. Games, walks, toys, or treats teach dogs that their actions earn rewards. In addition, they also establish your position as leader.

Leadership doesn't mean getting power over your dog. Instead, leadership accepts that successful housetraining is a duet, not a solo. Sometimes like a round robin in choral singing, it requires other people such as friends, family, or pet walkers to help carry the melody. Yet no matter how many voices sing, there is just one individual who leads the group, and that's you.

With housetraining, once the active schooling program is over, you should still reward the dog for a puddle or pile in the right place occasionally. Not every day, or every time, but you never want the dog to forget that the leader appreciates her decision to target the doggy toilet area. Although by this time the reward is strictly verbal, the enthusiasm in your voice shows your pleasure, pride, and happiness at her actions. Verbal praise is easy to give, requires no extra effort, and motivates your dog to perform those behaviors that make her a winner in your eyes.

Idea #4: Follow the Gemini Rule

The common lament among frustrated doggy toilet trainers is "I only stopped watching the dog for a couple of seconds when I opened the refrigerator door, answered the phone, or looked at my daughter's homework . . ." Accidents happen when your attention wanders.

To appreciate the significance of two seconds, ask a person who avoided a car crash. To recognize the importance of one second, ask a racehorse trainer whose horse won second place. To realize the value of a millisecond, ask a swimmer who won the silver at the Olympics.

Paying attention requires more than your physical presence; it also demands mental awareness. If you cannot watch your dog while you wash dishes, change what you are doing or move the dog to his den.

You can't go wrong if you follow the Gemini Rule. You are Castor; the dog is Pollux. You were single, now you are a pair. Like twins, you are his shadow; day or night you are near him. The secret to his behavior is to stick close. You cannot teach a dog if you are not with him.

Idea #5: Practice Canine Courtesy Customs

I encountered my first Canine Courtesy Custom when I worked with an enormous bull mastiff many years ago. Once I recognized the existence of habits, thoughts, and activities that over time established a certain custom, it seemed that every handler and dog I worked with would add to, share, or refine them. The following list results from my interactions with an exotic Chinese crested, a friendly Clumber spaniel, an eight-week-old Welsh corgi, a five-year-old English setter, and many others. Practicing Canine Courtesy has become a way of life to me. Canine Courtesy Customs ask you to look at dogs in new ways, develop different habits, change your thinking, focus on another aspect of activities, and establish new traditions. And there are still more customs waiting to be discovered.

CANINE COURTESY CUSTOMS

Put "play with dog" at the top of your list of things to do today.
That way, at least you will enjoy part of your day.

Dogs come in many sizes, colors, weights, and heights;
pick one that fits you.

If your dogs want to be near you, enjoy it. It means
they need you.

A dog doesn't need any coaxing to be your best friend.

If you can't play with your dog, he will wait. But if you don't
play with your dog, you don't know what you are missing.

Your dog needs you; take time to see him.

Why is there no organization called Dogaholics Anonymous?
Because no one wants to quit.

A friendly lick can provide your total daily allowance of love.

If all your schooling time is fun time, does that mean
you no longer have to "work" the dog?

Puddles and piles in the house are a dog's way of showing
that he needs more training.

Be patient with your dog and he will be patient with you.

Forgive your dog and he will ignore it when you make a mistake.

It takes less time to teach dogs to do it right the first time.

It doesn't matter how many days the housetraining takes; do
what's best for the relationship.

Don't get mad at your dog. She's not disobedient,
she's ignorant. Teach her.

If you want to forget all your troubles, play with a puppy.

The quickest way to double your time is to find someone
to help you.

When the going gets tough, the tough laugh.

Never miss a chance to praise your dog.

If you find yourself in a jam, make toast.

Dogs don't worry about you, they believe in you.

If we were like dogs, no one would ever be lonely.

Relationships happen while you work on other things.

You are never too old to play ball.

Practice canine courtesy, dogs will love you for it.

Don't give up. Your dog can do it!

Index

® **PLUME**

ALSO OF INTEREST

CATCH YOUR DOG DOING SOMETHING RIGHT *How to Train Any Dog in Five Minutes a Day*—Krista Cantrell Whatever your dog's age, breed, temperament, or social skills, *Catch Your Dog Doing Something Right* will help take the frustration out of dog training forever. It is the Ideal book for busy dog owners.

0-452-27755-8

THE NATURAL DOG *A Complete Guide for Caring Owners*—Mary L. Brennan, D.V.M., with Norma Eckroate *The Natural Dog* is the only complete guide to holistic health care for dogs available. Veterinarian Dr. Mary Brennan provides warm, understanding, and essential information on keeping pets well-behaved, superbly groomed, and in optimal health, with a natural approach to vaccinations, heartworm prevention, parasites, and skin problems.

0-452-27019-7

 **PLUME**

REMARKABLE ANIMALS

CLARA: THE EARLY YEARS *The Story of the Pug Who Ruled My Life*—**Margo Kaufman** "Before Clara, I was not a Pet Parent. The pugs were dogs. Cute dogs, willful dogs, lovable dogs to be sure, but I was a Human. I was in charge. Then along came Clara, and all bets were off."—Margo Kaufman. Filled with the author's trademark wit and wry observations, *Clara* is the hilarious and heartwarming story of an unforgettable pug—and her owner.

0-452-28136-9

STRANGE TAILS *All-Too-True News from the Animal Kingdom*—**John J. Kohut & Roland Sweet** From primates running in primaries to drunk and disorderly donkeys; from fowl play to feline fetishes; from birdbrains to the furry folk who make monkeys out of all of us, after reading the true stories in *Strange Tails* you'll never look at your pets the same way again

0-452-28118-0

ANGEL ANIMALS *Exploring Our Spiritual Connection with Animals*—**Allen and Linda Anderson** An insightful volume of inspirational animal stories—ranging from dogs and cats to raccoons and bears—which demonstrates how to recognize the interconnectedness of all living things.

0-452-28072-9